HOW TO MARKET AND SELL YOUR

ART
MUSIC
PHOTOGRAPHS
AND HANDMADE CRAFTS
ONLINE

TURN YOUR HOBBY INTO A CASH MACHINE

By Lee Rowley

How to Market and Sell Your Art, Music, Photographs, and Handmade Crafts Online: Turn Your Hobby Into a Cash Machine

Copyright © 2008 by Atlantic Publishing Group, Inc.
1405 SW 6th Ave. • Ocala, Florida 34471 • 800-814-1132 • 352-622-1875—Fax
Web site: www.atlantic-pub.com • E-mail: sales@atlantic-pub.com
SAN Number: 268-1250

ISBN-13: 978-1-60138-146-0   ISBN-10: 1-60138-146-8

Library of Congress Cataloging-in-Publication Data

Rowley, Lee, 1973-
   How to market and sell your art, music, photographs, and handmade crafts online : turn your hobby into a cash machine / by Lee Rowley.
      p. cm.
   Includes bibliographical references and index.
   ISBN-13: 978-1-60138-146-0 (alk. paper)
   ISBN-10: 1-60138-146-8 (alk. paper)
   1. Electronic commerce. 2. Internet marketing. 3. Selling--Handicraft. 4. Handicraft--Marketing. I. Title.

   HF5548.32.R687 2008
   745.5068'8--dc22
                                    2008005885

INTERIOR LAYOUT DESIGN: Vickie Taylor • vtaylor@atlantic-pub.com

Printed in the United States   Printed on Recycled Paper

Table of Contents

Introduction

Starving artist is a cliché that reminds us of society's opinion of people in the creative fields or, more accurately, of their ability to make a decent living from pursuing their arts. As a creative person, you have probably been told by well-intentioned but misguided friends, family members, career counselors, and teachers that, while creative pursuits are nice as hobbies, they are no way to make a living.

This is precisely the reason so many talented artists, crafters, photographers, and musicians spend their days working at jobs they do not like and in environments that do not inspire them or feed their creative natures. We are taught that art and music are not real jobs, so we settle for something that bores us, stifles us, and relegates our creative endeavors to hobby status.

Fortunately, there are now more opportunities than ever for

artistic people to realize their dreams of making a living from their creative works. The Internet has opened up a whole new world for artists and craftspeople alike — a world in which creative people have endless opportunities to be seen and heard, no matter where they live or to whom they are connected. Artists no longer have to live in one of the world's major metropolitan areas to have a chance at artistic success, neither do they have to be represented by a well-known agent. A musician in rural Idaho can run a successful Internet business just as effectively as a musician living in Los Angeles, and an artist in Copenhagen can sell as many paintings online as an artist in New York City.

Although the Internet has been instrumental in leveling the playing field for artists, selling creative works online is no longer as simple as it once was. In the early days of the Internet, an artist could simply put together a basic Web site and upload a few pictures, and visitors would come, browse, and buy. Now that the Internet has surpassed magazines, newspapers, and even television as our primary source of information, competition for online sales among artists, crafters, and musicians has increased exponentially. As a result, it has become more difficult for individual artists to establish a visible presence online.

To illustrate this point, let us look at one of the most common ways Internet users find Web sites that contain the items they are looking for — search engine queries. Using a search engine, such as those found on Google, MSN, or Yahoo!, is simple. Internet users type in a few words that capture the essence of what they are looking for, and the search engine returns a list of Web sites that, according to the Web site's content, contain relevant items.

With that in mind, here are some search terms and the number of relevant items taken from Google that people use to search for creative works:

- Abstract art — 10,200,000

- Art photography — 23,100,000

- Country music — 66,600,000

- Cubist painting — 273,000

- Handmade crafts — 1,110,000

- Independent music — 15,700,000

- Landscape art — 58,600,000

- Rock music — 55,100,000

- Stock photography — 28,700,000

These numbers may seem a little surprising, but they are real numbers that reflect the sheer volume of Web sites trying to attract the same visitors and turn them into customers. This intense competition shows that more artists than ever have discovered the power of the Internet as a marketing and sales vehicle.

Do not let these numbers scare you away from setting up your art business online, though. The good news (for you, anyway) is the vast majority of these creative souls do not know how to use the Internet to its fullest potential. For each search term, there are only a handful of Web sites that are able to effectively attract a steady stream of visitors. These are the ones that appear on the first few pages of the search results and especially those that appear on the first page.

Getting a Web site into one these top positions is no accident. It requires careful planning, a bit of research, and a specific goal that carries through all aspects of building your business online.

To be successful selling creative works on the Internet today, a crafter, photographer, or musician cannot simply rely on the fact that he or she is adept at creating art that is pleasing to the senses. An artist must also be a skilled businessperson and must understand the nuances of attracting visitors and converting them into paying customers. Without approaching online sales with this sort of keen focus, you are unlikely to operate a successful art business on the Internet.

This is why this book was created. It would take an artist years to learn how to properly use the Internet as a marketing vehicle and discover all the resources necessary to make an online art business profitable. Working artists do not have the time to endure the trial-and-error process while they are trying to make money online with their creative works. They need a resource to provide them with a blueprint to success so they can spend more time creating and less time analyzing marketing errors. That blueprint is contained within these pages.

This book is a guide to understanding how to use the Internet to market and sell art, music, photographs, and crafts. It is not a collection of vague theory, nor does it presuppose a reader already possesses a certain level of knowledge about Internet marketing. Instead, it starts at the beginning and provides specific, step-by-step instructions to create, maintain, and expand a successful online business.

Within these pages you will learn:

- How to select the right computer and other hardware

- How to use software programs to help you build your clientele

- How to create a Web site that showcases your creative works, has a professional look and feel, and makes visitors comfortable with the idea of buying from you

- How to use low cost and free advertising to drive visitors to your Web site

- How to use online auctions to gain rapid sales

- How to use other Web sites to promote your artworks, crafts, photographs, and music

You will also learn how to accept payments online so you do not have to go through the tedious task of matching up mailed checks with orders for artworks and many other tips that will help you build a successful online business.

You hold in your hands the key to becoming successful online as a creative businessperson. It will take hard work and a fair amount of patience to accomplish this, but, if you follow the steps, tips, and techniques described in this book, you will have a tremendous advantage that you can use to make art not only your hobby, but also your career.

Let us begin with the first question that an artist must pose when embarking on a career of selling creative works on the Internet: "Why sell online?"

Why Sell Online?

Ask the average person what he or she envisions when thinking of a successful artist, and he or she may tell you about paintings hanging in a gallery or sculptures placed on white block stands while the artist mills about, wearing black and drinking expensive lattes. Ask the same person about craftspeople, and the response may entail people selling handmade crafts at flea markets and county fairs. Ask about musicians, and his or her mind will conjure up images of professional recording studios and CDs lining the shelves of record stores.

What people do not think of is an artist running a Web site with frequent visitors and brisk sales or a musician with a large body of musical works available for download. The Internet is still on the periphery of segments of the public's mind, especially among those who claim to take art seriously. However, as noted in the introduction, the Internet now plays a crucial part in the marketing, sales, and display of artistic works.

For the artist, musician, or crafter, there are several distinct advantages to establishing a presence in the online marketplace. You have the ability to reach a global marketplace; you can reach millions of people for a fraction of the advertising cost needed to reach an offline audience; and you can sell your works much more quickly than you could if you were selling art or music offline.

Reaching a Global Audience

Let us consider two artists: One artist, preferring the traditional method of selling his or her artworks, submits proposals to art gallery owners, enters works into local and regional art shows, and develops print advertising to reach potential customers. The other, understanding the power of the Internet to market and sell artworks, develops and implements a marketing plan based on a business Web site, online auctions, networking with other online artists, and regular e-mail promotions.

The traditional marketer will spend a considerable amount of time writing query letters to art galleries and filling out entry forms for upcoming art shows. He or she will also invest considerable time in developing print marketing — flyers, postcards, press releases, and business cards. For all this effort, the artist will be rewarded with the capacity to reach a relatively small audience. This audience consists of the people who are inclined to respond to advertisements for fine arts, crafts, and photography; the people who wander through the galleries where artworks hang; and the people who attend the art shows to which his or her paintings have been accepted.

The online marketer will also spend a substantial amount of

time developing marketing materials — an attractive and easily navigable Web site, artwork photographs and descriptions, and promotional articles and Web log posts. Unlike the traditional marketing artist, though, he or she will have the opportunity to have his or her artworks seen by not just hundreds or even thousands of people, but literally millions of potential customers all over the world. People who would never think of setting foot in a brick-and-mortar art gallery or craft mall will happily go online to browse for a new painting for the home or office, handmade crafts to decorate a living room, or a framed photograph to hang in the library.

These are people who may not feel comfortable inside an art gallery but who still appreciate original, unique arts and crafts. They may not be the target market for high-end gallery owners, but they can certainly be your target market.

Aside from the ability to reach millions of potential buyers each day, having a global presence online gives a working artist several key advantages.

The Internet Never Closes

An artist marketing his or her creative works online does not have to deal with the constraints of typical gallery or studio hours. Artworks can be purchased online any time of the day or night, and the artist does not even have to be in front of the computer to complete the sale. This means that while you are sleeping, not only can night owls in your country see and purchase your artworks, but people halfway across the world who are going about their daily routine at that time can also buy your art.

People Have Different Tastes in Art

When an artist markets through a gallery in a local area, he or she is limited by the tastes, attitudes, and opinions of the local culture. For example, if you paint artworks that draw influence from surrealism but the local community is primarily interested in impressionism, you likely will not have much success marketing your artworks locally. You will need to either change the style and subject matter of your artwork or be content with enjoying your artwork in your own home.

When you market via the Internet, you are not constrained by the tastes and preferences of the local art-buying public. It does not matter if the style and subject matter of your artistic works are not in line with your local community's tastes and preferences, because you will be able to reach people in other states and even other countries. Although your artwork may not appeal to people in your home town, it will appeal to someone, and that person may be in the next town over or several time zones away.

For example, one artist living in the Midwestern United States found that a series of his paintings, characterized by rich textures, abstract patterns, and bright colors, received a cool reception in his home state. By marketing online, however, he noticed a large percentage of works from this series found buyers in Mexico. Had he stuck with traditional offline marketing, he would have never found this pool of buyers for that series of paintings.

A global audience creates more opportunities to reach different types of buyers.

An artist in his or her hometown may be limited to a certain type of buyers for creative works, such as renters or homeowners looking for artworks or crafts to display in a residence or individual buyers seeking to purchase a CD for personal use. Although these certainly represent viable markets for an artist, they are not the only ones that may benefit from access to creative works. A global presence gives an artist access to not only individuals, but small businesses looking for artwork to display in office waiting rooms or reception areas or corporations seeking large works to display in lobbies, company cafeterias, board rooms, and employee work areas. Similarly, the worldwide presence available through Internet marketing gives a musician the opportunity to attract clients seeking music to use in advertisements or other promotional materials.

Minimizing Advertising Costs

Another major advantage of marketing online is you can reach a large number of potential customers with a much smaller advertising cost than if you marketed to customers offline. Online advertising can be a cost-effective way to reach the people who want to buy your artworks, crafts, photographs, and music.

With traditional marketing of creative works, an artist can spend a significant amount of money on the design, printing, and distribution of business cards, postcards, flyers, and other printed marketing materials. For example, even if you choose one of the many all-inclusive services available on the Internet, such as **www.cheep-cheep.com**, the cost to print 5,000 art postcards can be nearly $2,000 — and that does not include postage. If you want to include several images on a folded brochure, the price can jump to almost $2,500.

In addition, some art galleries charge hanging fees or display fees for each piece of artwork placed on display in the gallery — these can range from $15 per artwork in smaller galleries in the Midwestern United States to well over $100 per artwork in a New York or Los Angeles gallery. Craft malls also charge fees for the rental of the space necessary to display craft items, although they do not charge a separate fee for the display of each item.

These fees do not include gallery commission amounts that are charged against the sale of each artwork that finds a buyer through a gallery. Gallery commissions are a percentage of the sale price of each artwork or craft item — they can be as much of 50 percent in some galleries.

It is easy to spend thousands of dollars building your presence in brick-and-mortar galleries with no guarantee you will be able to make the money back through the sale of your creative works.

Let us compare this with marketing your creative works online. The cost of registering the domain name for your Web site may be between $10 and $20, and some Web site hosting providers, such as **www.ibuilt.net** and **www.ixwebhosting.com,** will waive the cost of registering your Web site's domain name when you purchase a hosting package through them.

The cost of hosting packages varies according to the features the hosting provider offers and the ability the Web site owner has to customize and update his or her site. Some providers, such as **www.godaddy.com**, offer basic hosting packages that you can purchase for less than $7 a month, as well as other hosting packages that include Web site design software and even professional Web site design. Other hosting providers offer more robust Web site design features, such as the ability to include forms to capture visitor contact information and deliver it to your e-mail in-box — **www.ibuilt.net** offers such services for $19.99 per month, and **www.sitekreator.com** offers a similar service for $29.99 per month.

Aside from your Web site, there are various art, craft, and music cooperative sites that you can subscribe to for a nominal fee. For example, **www.ebsqart.com** gives you access to exclusive online art shows, artist community bulletin boards, charity events, and contests for $7.50 per month.

If you are willing to take the time to do some research, you can also use pay-per-click search engine marketing to help bring customers to your Web site. Realistically, you can spend as much or as little for this type of advertising as you want, but if you bid on the right keywords, you can gain exposure for as little as five cents per click.

There are also marketing techniques you can implement for free, such as writing online blogs, participating in discussion board threads, writing articles for online directories, building links to your Web site, and optimizing the content of your Web site so it will appear high in the rankings of search engines such as Google, MSN, Yahoo!, and others. Chapters 4 and 5 of this book provide a wealth of information on how to use these techniques to increase visibility and drive traffic to your Web site.

It is possible to build a well-crafted online marketing strategy for less than $100 per month — even less if you are willing to do some of the work involved in creating your own Web site and optimizing it for high search engine rankings. You would be hard pressed to develop an effective advertising strategy for this amount in the traditional offline marketing world, but online, it is possible.

Selling Your Artwork Quickly

Art galleries move works rather slowly, partially because of the lack of significant daily traffic through the gallery's doors and partially because people tend to just browse when they are visiting a gallery. Craft malls and music stores share the same challenge — for every craft item or CD that sells on a given day, there are perhaps hundreds of others still awaiting a buyer. Unless they are displaying your works entirely on consignment, art gallery owners and craft mall owners are not particularly motivated to sell your art, because you are already paying them for the privilege of displaying your creative works in their retail spaces.

When you sell your creative works online, you are in control of how quickly you sell your art. It may take time to build a steady stream of traffic for your Web site, but there are several ways you can use the Internet to achieve impressive sales while you are building a loyal customer base online.

The first way is through using online auctions. Although you are using search engine marketing, blogging, and other tools to attract visitors to your Web site, you can also use auctions to sell artworks within a matter of days — sometimes you will find buyers have placed bids on an artwork before the paint is even dry.

Another way that online marketing can help you enjoy frequent sales as an artist is by allowing you to display more artworks on a single Web site than you ever could in a physical gallery. You can have hundreds of artworks, craft items, or photographs available for sale at the same time, which gives your visitors plenty to choose from — they are not limited to the small number of works that a gallery owner or craft mall manager is willing to let you display. Even during your initial traffic-building phase, more choices means more sales.

A third way you can use the Internet to increase the speed and frequency of your sales is by displaying your artwork in many different places at one time. If you are hanging your art in a physical gallery, that is the only place people can see it; however, when you are selling that same artwork online, you can display it on your Web site, in an online auction, on your blog, on an artist's cooperative Web site such as **www.deviantart.com**, and in discussion board postings (if permitted by the discussion board moderator).

Now let us move on to the next chapter of this book, which will cover the first topic of learning how to successfully sell your works online — selecting the right hardware, software, and support for your online business.

2

The Basics: What You Will Need to Sell Your Products Online

Before you can start building and implementing the marketing tools you will need to build a successful and profitable Internet business, you will need to obtain a number of physical tools. This chapter will outline the basic components you will need to launch your Internet business.

Your Computer

Before you can start an online business, you will need to purchase a computer. Even if you have access to a computer at work or through your public library, it is unlikely you will be able to use it for the number of hours you will need to establish a viable online presence.

Even if you already own a computer, it is a good idea to evaluate your system's performance capabilities to ensure it will be able to handle the tasks you will need it to carry out. This is especially true if your computer is more than a few years old — technology quickly becomes obsolete, and you may find an older system is unable to handle the advanced Internet applications required to build a successful online business.

Before you purchase a new computer, though, you will need to know what to look for — not in terms of brand name, but in terms of the capabilities of a particular computer system. Different computer configurations are designed to handle different types of tasks, and unless you take the time to assess your particular needs, you could either wind up with a system that has insufficient capabilities or pay too much for a system that has features and power you will never use.

For the purposes of this section, "computer" refers to the components inside a computer case or laptop. Monitors, printers, and other peripheral hardware devices will be covered later in this chapter.

Here are the components you will need to consider when purchasing a new computer system:

Hard Drive

This is the component of your computer where your images, documents, music files, and software files are stored. The capacity of a hard drive is expressed in gigabytes (GB). Currently, internal hard drives are available with storage capacities ranging from 40 GB to 500 GB or more. The larger the storage capacity of your computer's hard drive, the more expensive it will be; however, choosing the largest hard drive you think you may ever need is a lot less expensive proposition than replacing your hard drive later.

Determining the hard drive capacity you will need involves a little guesswork, along with some knowledge of how much space different file types will occupy on your hard drive. Here are a few examples to help you get an idea of typical file sizes:

- A 10-page text-only document written in Microsoft Word will occupy roughly 50 kilobytes (KB) of space — that is 0.00005 GB. This means you could save 100,000 pages of text to your hard drive and still only take up 1 GB of disk space.

- A high-resolution image that measures 1,000 pixels x 1,600 pixels will take up between 1 megabyte (MB) and 3 MB of disk space. This means you can store between 300 and 1,000 images of this size and resolution on 1 GB of your hard drive's disk space.

- Software applications vary in the amount of space they occupy. Adobe Acrobat Reader 8.1, which allows you to open and view PDF files (documents designed to be readable but not editable), will occupy 32.6 MB on your hard drive; in comparison, Dreamweaver CS3, a software application that allows you to design your own Web sites, takes up nearly 1.3 GB of space.

If you plan on designing your own Web sites, using graphics

software such as Adobe Photoshop® or Corel Paint Shop Pro, or storing large amounts of photo images on your computer, you should look for a computer with at least an 80 GB hard drive. Choosing an even larger hard drive, such as a 150 GB or even a 300 GB drive, can help ensure you will not have to upgrade your computer for several years.

If it is in your budget, it is also a good idea to purchase an external hard drive to back up all your image, text, and software files. By using an external drive for backup, you will not have to worry about losing your important files if your computer crashes or losing access to them when your operating system becomes corrupted.

Memory Card

This is an internal computer component that provides RAM (Random Access Memory) to run the processes on your computer, such as your operating system, software applications, Internet browser windows, and maintenance applications, such as virus scanners and anti-spyware programs.

The power of memory cards is expressed in MB or GB. The more power your memory card has, the faster your processes will run and the more processes you can run at the same time. A few years ago, a 256 MB memory card was sufficient to run an operating system (such as Windows or Linux), with enough memory left over to run several other processes. With the release of more robust operating systems, however, at least a 512 MB memory card is recommended (and, with the recent release of Windows Vista, required) to run the processes on your computer.

If you want to be able to run multiple processes on your computer, such as photo editors, web browser windows, and word processing applications, it is a good idea to purchase a memory card with more than 1 GB of memory. Cards are commonly available with 2 GB to 8 GB of memory, which can help ensure that your computer does not freeze while you are busy building your business.

Processor

A computer's processor (or CPU) acts as the gateway for all your computer's functions. As its name suggests, it is responsible for processing all the data used to make your audio, video, and software applications run smoothly.

There are three main manufacturers of computer processors today: Intel, AMD, and Cyrix. Of these, Intel processors are the most commonly used in personal computers sold as packages through vendors like **www.dell.com** and **www.gateway.com**.

Intel's Celeron processors are used in less expensive computer packages because they are built to handle fewer computer functions at once and process data at speeds that, while acceptable for home users for browsing the Internet or creating Word documents, may not be acceptable for people using home computers for numerous concurrent processes or intense graphics or video applications.

Intel provides a higher-end line of processes under the Pentium name. These processors offer faster processing speeds, the ability to run more processes at once, and enhanced graphics and multimedia support.

AMD and Cyrix processors are less commonly used in packaged systems, but if you are building your own computer or having someone else build it for you, both brands offer processors that will be able to handle all your Web site building, traffic monitoring, and sales tasks.

If your business-building tasks will be limited to simple Web design and image uploading and you do not mind slightly slower processing speeds, you can get away with using a Celeron processor. If, on the other hand, you will be extensively using graphics programs such as Photoshop® or Paint Shop Pro or you will be using video or other multimedia to enhance your business Web site, a Pentium processor will give you the speed and power you need to handle these applications.

CD-ROM, CD-RW, or DVD-R Drive

To install software onto your computer, you will need to have at least a CD-ROM drive.

If you will be using more than one computer for your business-building activities, it is a good idea to have a CD-RW drive, which will allow you to copy files to a blank disk so you can transfer the files from one computer to another. This can also help you with offline marketing, because you can make CDs that contain digital galleries of your works which you can send to prospective clients, galleries, or craft malls for evaluation or contest submission.

An even more versatile option is a DVD-R drive, which will allow you to create DVDs of movies showcasing your works, video artist biographies, and other promotional materials.

Video Card

This is the component of your computer that acts as an interface between your computer and your display monitor, generating video images that can be displayed on the system's monitor. The better the quality of your video card, the better the quality of the displayed images and the smoother video files will play on your computer.

The capacity of a video card to handle images and streaming video is expressed in MB. This refers to the video file size that a video card can process at any given time without tapping into the computer's RAM. Cards are currently available from 128 MB to 768 MB, although cards with less than 256 MB of memory are becoming difficult to find.

If you will be selling artworks, crafts, or photographs online, it is a good idea to purchase a computer with at least a 512 MB video card — this will give you the image quality you need to enhance photographs to display on your Web site, online auctions, and blogs.

Sound Card

The sound card is the computer component that acts as an interface between your computer and external sound output devices, such as computer speakers or a stereo system. The better the quality of your sound card, the better the quality of the audio output from your speakers.

If you are a musician who will be selling your songs online, a high-quality sound card is essential, because it allows you to make sure your uploaded music files are as clear and balanced as possible. Having a high-quality sound card also optimizes your use of music mixing software, which will allow you to adjust the various levels of your recording, edit parts of your songs, and create remixes of popular song tracks.

Computer Packages

The easiest way to purchase a computer that meets all your needs for running a successful online business is to purchase a computer package from one of the many online or offline vendors that specialize in creating and selling packaged units designed to fit specific budgets and applications.

The advantages of purchasing a packaged computer system are threefold. First, you will not have to find and price each individual component of your computer separately. This can take up quite a bit of time, not only to select the correct components, but to make sure each component is compatible with the other elements of your computer system.

Second, purchasing a packaged computer can save you a substantial amount of money over purchasing individual components. Companies that offer computer packages know you will not be buying just a sound card or a CD drive from them —

you will be buying every necessary component of your computer. Because they are getting all your business instead of just a piece of it, they can offer you the entire package at a discounted price.

Third, you will not have to assemble the computer yourself or pay someone to come to your home and assemble it for you. When your computer unit is shipped to you, you will need to connect all your peripherals (described in the next section of this chapter), turn your computer on, and it will be ready to use in a matter of minutes.

A variety of computer packages designed to meet nearly any user's needs are available through businesses such as **www.dell. com**. This Web site offers several configurations for both desktop and laptop computers, and you can customize your computer package to add, remove, or upgrade components before your computer is built. That way, if you anticipate you will need a hard drive with a larger storage capacity or more RAM to run multiple applications at once, you can do this with the click of a mouse. You can also select peripherals for your computer and receive a complete package that you can use to quickly get your business up and running.

Dell offers special pricing on at least one of its computer packages almost every day of the year. These specials change frequently, so if you are willing to wait for a week or two to purchase your computer, you have a good chance of getting a better deal than if you simply made a quick purchase. Some of these special pricing deals come in the form of free shipping or free upgrades, so it pays to be somewhat flexible in your timing and your system requirements.

You can also find similar purchasing flexibility at **www.gateway.com.** This Web site offers a similar process for selecting and purchasing your computer and also offers free upgrades and peripherals, such as purchasing incentives on some models.

If you do not have loyalty to a particular brand, shop around on these Web sites and check prices with other online and offline vendors. If you are willing to do a bit of shopping around, you can pick up a basic desktop or laptop computer for under $500, and that price includes a monitor for desktop units. Although the prices of the low-end packages are attractive, they may not provide you with the power you need to run your online business. If you have read the component descriptions in this section, you should have a good idea of which components to upgrade. It is easier (and less expensive) to upgrade components before your computer is built than it is to order upgrade components after you receive your computer package.

Your Peripherals

Now that you have selected the specifications for your computer, let us look at the peripheral devices that will help you build your online business.

Monitor

Purchasing a high-quality monitor will go a long way toward helping you create images of your artworks, handmade crafts, and photographs that make your creative works come to life on a potential customer's computer screen. It is difficult to see the nuances of your digital images on a small, low-quality monitor, particularly if you are photographing detailed artworks or crafts.

Because your Web site and auction listings do not allow visitors to see, touch, and feel the quality of your artworks, they have to rely on the digital images of these items when evaluating them and making a decision as to whether to purchase. Your images must be clear, undistorted, and free of distracting shadows and glare. Even the most stunning artworks do not have much of a chance of being sold online if the images of the work are fuzzy, grainy, or poorly lit.

A large, high-quality monitor will help you spot flaws in these images and will be indispensable for using image enhancement programs, such as Adobe Photoshop®, TruView PhotoFlair, or AutoFX.

Digital Camera

Purchasing a digital camera is essential to creating images that will help sell your artwork. Although it is possible to take photos with a traditional 35mm camera and have them scanned to image files on a CD or on your computer's hard drive, this is a time consuming and potentially costly endeavor, and you will lose a significant amount of picture quality during the scanning process.

When choosing a digital camera to take pictures of your artworks or craft items, you should look for a camera that can produce crisp, high-resolution images and that is simple to operate. Here are a few things to look for in a digital camera:

- **High megapixel capacity.** One-megapixel images are fine for taking pictures of your Las Vegas vacation to e-mail to your friends and coworkers, but if you try to enlarge images with this resolution to a size greater than 400 x 600 pixels, you will quickly see the poor quality of these images. This is because as you enlarge the pictures, the photo software does not have sufficiently detailed information to reproduce the image accurately in larger sizes. To compensate for this lack of detailed digital information, the software will pixelate the image, that is, turn areas of your image into visibly noticeable blocks of color, rather than reproducing a true image.

  To create accurate, detailed images of your creative works that can be enlarged to 800 by 1200 pixels or larger, you will need a digital camera with no less than a 6-megapixel capacity. Cameras are now available with more than 12 megapixel capacity, which can produce images that can not only be used in online marketing, but also flyers and posters for offline marketing as well.

- **Optical zoom.** Nearly every digital camera today has a zoom feature that lets you take close-up shots without moving closer to the subject you are photographing. When you are shopping for a digital camera, it is important to note whether a particular model features optical zoom or digital zoom.

  Digital zoom crops and enlarges an image digitally, which can cause the same sort of pixilation that occurs when you enlarge a low-resolution image on your computer. Again, this may be fine for taking pictures of the Eiffel Tower from afar, but it will not do you any good when you are trying to create images that will make your artworks sell.

Optical zoom, on the other hand, works by physically distancing the lenses within the camera, much like a traditional 35mm film camera. This allows you to create a close-up image that is undistorted and free from the pixilation caused by digital zoom features.

Some cameras have both optical zoom and digital zoom features. If you are planning to use your digital camera for family vacations as well as for creating images of your artworks to use on your Web site and auction listings, this may be a good choice for you.

- **Point-and-shoot functionality.** If you are planning to make selling art, crafts, or photographs online your career, you will want to spend as much time as possible creating art and as little time as possible creating images of your works. Complicated cameras with numerous manual functions are fine for the true photography enthusiast, but for the purpose of creating images as marketing tools, it is a good idea to stick with point-and-shoot models that will allow you to photograph your creative works quickly and easily.

Here are several options that will give you the power and flexibility you need to take photos of your creative works (or even make your photos the creative works themselves) that will stand out online:

- If economy is your primary concern, an HP Photosmart M547 is available for about $80 at **www.circuitcity.com**. This digital camera will give you enough power to take quality photographs, with its 5-megapixel capacity and 3x optical zoom. You will need to upload your images fairly frequently, though, since it comes with a rather small 16 MB memory card.

- A more feature-rich but still affordable option is the Canon Powershot 7.1 megapixel camera. It is small enough to take anywhere, yet it is capable of producing high-resolution images suitable for online use. It also features 3x optical zoom for getting detailed shots of your works without loss of image clarity. You can pick up this camera from **www.bestbuy.com** for around $250.

- If getting professional-quality images from a professional camera is your objective, you could step up to the Olympus E-210 EVOLT, which features 10 megapixel capacity, auto focus in live mode, and an integrated TruePic III processor for improved image quality and less noise. There are also two separate zoom lenses available (the ZUIKO 14 — 42 mm and the ZUIKO 40 — 150 mm) to accommodate nearly any imaging situation imaginable. The camera retails for about $750 at **www.pcconnection.com.**

Video Camera

In recent years, videos on the Internet have emerged as one of the hottest elements of Web site content available. People love to watch videos, and it has become quite easy to upload files from a video camera and embed them on your Web site.

Although embedded video is by no means a required element, it is a good way to keep your Web site visitors around longer so they will be more likely to purchase from you. Here are some options to consider:

- If you are looking for a budget-priced digital video camera, an excellent choice is the Panasonic PV GS80, available from **www.buydig.com** for less than $300. Although this camera offers little in the way of effects for your video, it is an economical unit that will provide adequate image quality for Internet video applications.

- A better choice that still will not break your budget is the Sony Handycam DCR-SR40. It may not impress video enthusiasts watching on a large-screen television, but it provides video quality that is more than sufficient for the Internet. An added bonus is that video is stored in the camera's internal 30 GB hard drive, instead of on a Mini-DV or a DVD-R, which means you will not have to constantly buy disks for the unit. You can pick up this model from **www.bwayphoto.com** for about $430.

- If being able to obtain superior-quality video in both daytime and nighttime situations is important, the Canon DC40 can provide superior-quality video in both situations. If you are shooting video of yourself painting in a basement studio or other low-light situations, this may be a good choice. This camera also features 10x optical zoom for obtaining close-up video shots of your work. This camera is available from **www.shopdigitalcorp.com** for about $600.

Audio Speakers

If you are a visual artist, a standard set of speakers, such as the ones packaged with average quality desktop computers, will serve you just fine. If you are a working online musician, though, a high-quality set of speakers is indispensable.

Here are a few of the choices available that will give you audio far superior to standard computer speakers but that will not cost you thousands of dollars:

- The Logitech Z-10 Interactive speaker system retails for less than $150 on **www.amazon.com**, yet it provides the clear, balanced sound essential to effective music editing. These speakers are compact enough to sit on your desktop without taking up much of your valuable workspace.

- You can make a larger investment in the Bose Companion 3 Multimedia speaker system, available for about $250 on **www.thrillingaudio.com**, to obtain even more depth and clarity in your music. This speaker system provides true, clean mid-range tones and highs and adequate bass to give you a true sense of sound contour.

- If you are serious about obtaining premium-quality sound

for your music editing and mixing sessions, one of the best choices is the Samson Resolv 65a Powered Studio Monitor System, which you can order from **www.audiogear.com** for about $300. The Resolve 65a system provides the full, balanced audio you need to mix vocals, drums, and keyboards.

Printer

Unless you are creating your own offline marketing materials, there is not much point in purchasing a high-resolution laser printer with 500-sheet capacity and duplexing capabilities. Your printer will be used primarily to print invoices, contracts, shipping labels, and other documents related to the sale or commission of creative works.

A simple, inexpensive inkjet printer will perform well for this purpose. You can purchase an inkjet printer at a computer store for a cost of between $75 and $150, and you can also get one as part of a computer package for even less.

Scanner

If you are selling small artworks or print photography online, using a scanner to create digital images of your works is an easier method than taking pictures of your works with a digital camera. You will obtain images that are correctly lighted with little effort, and you will not have to worry about keystoning (an unwanted effect that occurs in your images when the artwork is not photographed straight on — the bottom or top of the artwork appears smaller or larger than the opposite edge in keystoned images).

For artworks and photographs less than 8.5" x 11" in size, a simple flatbed scanner is ideal. A flatbed scanner has a large glass plate on which pictures are placed for scanning and a flat hinged lid that holds the picture against the glass to prevent curling or ripples. The result is a clean, neatly centered image that makes your artwork stand out.

Scanners with automatic document feeders provide quicker scanning speeds, but if a photograph or artwork becomes jammed in the feeder, your art can be ruined. If you have a scanner with an automatic document feeder, it is best to avoid using the feeder to scan fine art.

Your Internet Service Provider

To build an online business, you will need a reliable Internet connection. Internet service providers (ISPs) offer several packages to meet your needs with prices that depend on the type and speed of the connection you choose.

If you are looking for a low cost solution for connecting to the Internet, the least expensive option is a dial-up connection. This type of connection uses your telephone line to transmit data via a phone cable that connects your computer to a telephone jack in your home. Your computer connects to the Internet by dialing a phone number designated by your ISP. Although this is an inexpensive solution (packages range from $8 to $20 per month), there are several drawbacks that may make this an ineffective long-term solution:

Loading Web pages is a slow (and occasionally impossible) process. Loading a simple text-only Web page can take several seconds on a dial-up connection. Add high-resolution images or Flash animation, and it can take 30 seconds or more to load a page.

The performance of a dial-up connection is affected by the number of people using a particular access phone number at one time. During peak usage periods, you will find your Internet access is extremely slow, and there may be times when so many people are accessing the Internet through the same dial-up number that you may not be able to connect to the Internet.

Uploading and downloading files is an even slower process. When you are building and updating a business Web site showcasing art, crafts, music files, or photographs, you will need to upload images to your Web site and download software applications to track sales and Web site statistics. A single image can take several minutes to upload; a software application can tie up your computer for an hour or more.

When you are connected to the Internet, your phone line is occupied. This means you will not be able to receive telephone calls while you are working on your Web site or reviewing customer orders. Not only does this make it difficult for your friends or family to contact you while you are online, it also makes it impossible for you to view a customer order online while you are discussing the order with a customer via the telephone.

A faster alternative to dial-up service is a broadband or high-speed Internet connection. This type of connection transmits data through a cable line rather than a telephone line and is capable of transmitting data 50 to 100 times faster than a dial-up connection. An added advantage of a high-speed Internet connection is that, because it does not use a telephone line to access the Internet, your phone line will be free while you are online.

High-speed Internet packages are significantly more expensive than dial-up connections — you can expect to pay $30 to $70 for this type of connection. If you purchase your telephone and cable or satellite television service through the same provider, you may be able to obtain a bundled package that includes high-speed Internet at a reduced monthly cost.

If you are using a laptop for your online business, you can use a wireless Internet card to connect to the Internet at stores and restaurants designated as Wi-Fi hotspots without an Internet package of your own. If you have a desktop computer in your home that already has a high-speed Internet connection, you can access the Internet on your laptop by connecting a router (a device that permits an Internet connection to laptops in or near your home) to your desktop computer.

You can also purchase a wireless or cellular Internet card for your laptop that allows online access through satellite transmission of Internet data — this allows you to connect from virtually anywhere, regardless of whether a standard wireless connection is available. These wireless cards are available through several Internet service providers, and service for these cards starts at about $80 per month.

3

Creating a Web Site: Establishing Your Presence in the Virtual World

Now that you have purchased the computer and peripherals that are right for your online business, the next step is to create a Web site to serve as the hub of your business. Creating a Web site can seem like a daunting task, but when you have the correct tools, it is quite easy to build and maintain an attractive, easily navigable Web site that will compel your visitors to purchase your artworks, craft items, photographs, or music.

This chapter will give you the information you need to build a Web site for your online business, even if you have never built a site before. You will learn how to reserve a name for your Web site, how to use templates to make your Web site building process quick and efficient, and how to make your Web site easy to navigate so your visitors can find the items they want to purchase.

Before we delve into the technical aspects of building a Web site, let us examine why it is crucial to the success of your business to have a fully functional Web site. There are several reasons:

- It establishes your credibility as an artist and a businessperson. Having a Web site shows you are serious about your career as an artist, musician, craftsperson, or photographer. It demonstrates a sense of professionalism that Internet users have come to expect, and it shows your customers you intend to remain on the Internet for many years to come, so your visitors will always be able to purchase your works and contact you with questions and commission requests. It also gives customers the sense that you are a serious businessperson interested in selling art and making sure that your customers are satisfied.

- It gives your customers the ability to purchase from you quickly and easily. By providing a hub for your online business, you give Web site visitors the opportunity to choose and purchase artwork, crafts, photographs, or music from your entire body of work. If a customer is looking for a particular creative work, your Web site is the first place they will look to find it.

- It increases your repeat business. Once a customer has purchased a creative work from your Web site, he or she will remember your Web site address for a long time to come. If you provide frequently changing content on your Web site (more on Web site content in Chapter 4), your customers and potential customers will have a reason to come back to your Web site time and time again. If you keep them coming back to your Web site, there is a good chance they will buy from you.

⊛ It is one of the least expensive forms of online advertising available. If you are willing to design the Web site yourself, you can easily launch a professional Web site for under $50. Once your Web site is finished and uploaded, there are several free and low cost ways to promote your Web site, so you can attract potential customers quickly.

With these reasons in mind, let us get started building your business Web site so you can attract visitors to view your creative works and start making money with your business.

Your Domain Name

Before you begin building your business Web site, you will need a domain name for your Web site. A domain name is the address that an Internet user types to access a particular Web site, for example, **www.google.com.**

Choosing a domain name is a tricky process, because it should reflect your personality as an artist, photographer, or musician while being short and catchy enough to remember easily. Not only that, but it must also be a domain name that is not already in use or registered to another person or business.

Using your name as your domain name works well if you already have an established following, but if you are new to the world of the Internet and do not have an offline client base that will visit your Web site, this is not the best way to attract visitors. If you want to use your name in your Web site address, use it in conjunction with other short words or phrases that accurately describe your business. For example, if John Smith wanted to build a Web site for his photography studio, www.JohnSmith-Photography.com would be a good choice for him to attract Web site visitors while building name recognition on the Internet.

A good way to test out domain names and determine whether they are available is to visit **www.godaddy.com**. There is a domain search function on GoDaddy's home page where you can enter potential domain names to check for availability. If a particular domain name is already taken, GoDaddy will suggest alternate domain names that are available.

Even if your domain name is available with an extension other than .com, such as .biz, .info, or .tv, it is important that you select a domain name with a.com extension. In the sometimes strange logic of the Internet, a domain name with an extension other than .com is widely perceived as being inferior or less professional, regardless of the quality of the design and content on the Web site.

Next, purchase and register the domain name through **a** hosting provider, and there are hundreds from which to choose. The cost of registering a domain name varies among hosting providers, but you can expect to pay less than $20 per year to reserve and use a domain name. If you purchase a hosting package and register a domain name with the same hosting provider, you may be able to obtain a domain name at a reduced cost. Domain name registration for .com extensions costs $8.99 per year through

www.godaddy.com, but if you purchase a hosting package, the name registration will cost you only $1.99 per year. Hosts such as **www.ixwebhosting.com** will give you three free domain name registrations when you buy a hosting package that supports up to eight Web sites. This can be a useful proposition if you create several different types of artwork or if you create not only artwork, but crafts and photography as well. You can also get free domain name registration through **www.ibuilt.net**, although the hosting packages are more expensive ($19.99 to 29.99 per month) because they offer more features.

Your Hosting Provider

A hosting provider is a company that places your Web site files on its servers (computers that hold a large amount of information) and allows visitors to access your Web site through its servers.

When choosing a hosting provider for your Web site, there are a number of things you should consider:

- **Storage space for your files.** As a person selling creative works online, you will be uploading numerous files to your Web site, such as images of your artworks, music files, and downloadable text files. If you are building a more robust Web site that includes Flash animation or video files, those will be stored on your hosting provider's servers as well.

  Hosting providers differ in the amount of file storage space they will allow per account. Three hosting packages available from **www.godaddy.com** provide 5 MB, 100 MB, or 200 MB of storage space. A hosting package available from **www.hostmonster.com** offers 300 MB of storage space.

- **File transfer allowance.** File transfer refers to the process of temporarily uploading the files that comprise your Web site to a visitor's Internet browser. If a visitor accesses a Web page that contains ten photographs that are 2 MB in size each, the file transfer size of those photographs is 20 MB. If the visitor visits ten similar pages on your Web site, 200 MB of your file transfer allowance are used.

  Your hosting provider will give you a monthly file transfer allowance. Once you have reached your monthly file transfer limit, the hosting provider will either charge you for transfers over your monthly allowance or suspend access to your Web site until the allowance is renewed.

  You may not be concerned about exceeding file transfer limits when you first launch a business Web site, but as your site grows in popularity, more people will visit your Web site on a regular basis. Choosing a provider that gives you a file transfer allowance of 1,000 GB or more will help to ensure you can keep the same hosting package for a year or more without upgrading.

- **Personalized e-mail addresses.** If you operate a Web site that sells creative works and a customer requests additional information, asks a question, or inquires about a purchase via e-mail, he or she would rather receive a response from yourname@yourWebsite.com than from a free account such as Gmail, Yahoo!, or Hotmail. Having an e-mail address that corresponds with your Web site address looks more professional and adds to the customer's opinion that you are serious about meeting his or her needs.

* **Site design software.** If you do not know HTML (the language in which Web sites are written) or you have never created a Web site before and do not want to spend much time designing it, you can use site design software offered by some hosting providers.

The type of Web site design software provided by Web site hosting companies allows you to choose from a collection of templates and then fill pre-set areas with text, images, links to other Web sites, and video files. The amount of control you have to customize the design of the templates varies — some software allows you to change the colors of the Web site but not the layout; other software allows you to alter both the colors and the layout. The more control you have over the look and feel of your Web site, the more expensive the hosting package will be.

Look for a hosting provider that gives out a demo of its design software; a video demo will give you a basic idea of how to use the software to create your site, but a limited free trial period will let you test out the software to see if it is simple to use and versatile. If a hosting provider does not offer a video demo or a free trial period, it is best to look elsewhere.

- ⊛ **CGI forms.** These are areas of a Web site where a visitor fills in his or her personal data to get more information about a product or to subscribe to a Web site's newsletter or e-mail list. When a visitor fills out a form and clicks the "Submit" button, the form sends the information to a program on the hosting company's server that translates the information into a format that can be sent to you via e-mail or used to populate a database.

  You can use the information you collect from these forms to build an e-mail list, which you can use to periodically contact your Web site visitors to notify them of new artworks, crafts, or music when it becomes available and to let them know about sales and special promotions.

Building Your Web Site

Once you have a domain name for your Web site and you have selected a provider to host your Web site files, you are ready to begin building a site to display and sell your creative works. The remainder of this chapter will give you tips and ideas for creating a Web site that is easy to navigate, is visually appealing to your visitors, and nets you the most sales.

Whether you use a template offered by a Web site design host or you use an advanced Web site building software package, such as Microsoft Expression Web (formerly Microsoft FrontPage) or Adobe Dreamweaver CS3 (formerly Adobe Dreamweaver 8), the first goal of building your business site should be to create a Web site that has a clean design and is easy to navigate. If you have a Web site that is not laid out in a logical manner, is cluttered with intricate background images or animation, or has links that are difficult to find, your visitors will quickly lose interest and move on to another Web site.

Here are the essential pages of an art-, craft-, or music-based Web site:

The Home Page

This is the first page that most people will see when they visit your Web site. For this reason, designing an effective home page is particularly important, because it will be the tool to attract the attention of Web site visitors and make them want to explore the other pages of your site.

The most important thing to know about building a home page for your Web site is that, because your site is about your creative works, your home page should focus on your art, not on your career as an artist or the professional logo you created for your art business.

It is understandable that a beginning Web site builder would want to place a logo, a picture of himself or herself, or a biography on the home page — these seem like logical choices for branding your art and adding a personal touch to a Web site. However, the best way to make your Web site visitors want to know more about you is to make them want to know more about your artwork, crafts, music, or photographs.

If you are a visual artist, make sure that an image of your best artwork is the first thing a visitor sees when your home page loads. It you are a craftsperson or a photographer, your best work should be placed front and center on your home page. If you are a musician, do not make your Web site visitors hunt for samples of your music — instead, place an embedded media player with your best song or composition near the top of your home page so visitors can hear your music right away.

There is nothing wrong with placing a logo on your business Web site's home page (or any page of your Web site, for that matter). Just do not overestimate your logo's importance in retaining Web site visitors — they came to your Web site to experience your creative genius, not to marvel at your fancy logo.

Also, make sure that links to your other pages are easy to find on your home page and throughout your Web site. The longer your visitors stay on your Web site, the more likely they are to buy from you — and letting them see your best work as soon as your site loads is the best way to make your visitors want to stay.

A Gallery of Your Creative Work

Aside from an effective home page, your gallery page is the best way to keep visitors on your site. Your gallery page should not include any extraneous images, text, or animation — this is a place for your visitors to focus solely on the works you have for sale.

Multiple gallery pages are fine if your artworks, crafts, or photographs can be easily divided into different categories. Just do not make your visitors click through too many Web site pages to find the creative works they are looking for.

If you have several gallery pages, one way to help streamline the navigation for your visitors is to build a gallery front page listing all your different art categories, with a sample image of each type of artwork for each category. You can even make the images link to your separate gallery pages, in addition to having the category descriptions link to the pages.

A Biography Page

Once your Web site visitors decide they like your work, they will naturally want to know more about you. This page lets your visitors know who you are, how you were drawn to the creative arts, and what you hope to convey through your works.

The biography page should also include your photograph so visitors can see the artist behind the work. A professional head shot gives you the appearance of being sincere and serious about your work and lends a personal touch to your Web site.

The biography page is an important tool in generating online sales because people like to buy from someone they feel like they know. Your written biography and your photograph help your Web site visitors feel connected to you, so they will be more inclined to trust you to treat them fairly, address their questions and concerns, and, most of all, provide them with unique, well-crafted works.

The Contact Page

This simple page should invite your visitors to contact you with questions, comments, and requests. You can also say your basic terms for commissioned works, so that people interested in hiring you to create a custom work will know whether you are available to create commissioned pieces and will understand your fee structure.

If your Web site hosting provider supports CGI, creating a simple CGI form on this page is the best way for your Web site visitors to contact you. It lets your visitors know what information you need to provide a response and cuts down on the number of unfocused and incomplete messages you receive in your e-mail inbox.

There are other pages you can add to your Web site, such as Frequently Asked Questions, Links (to other Web sites or your online auctions), and Recently Sold works. These pages help add content to your Web site, giving your visitors more to look at, but they are not essential to creating a Web site that will sell. If you are pressed for time or you simply want to keep your site simple, you can still build a professional business Web site without these pages.

Once you have decided on the number of pages for your Web site and have determined what each page will be about, you are ready to design the Web site itself. The remainder of this chapter focuses on the elements of your Web site's pages and gives you tips for designing a Web site that will appeal to your visitors.

Background Textures and Images

You may be tempted to use a textured background or use a picture or computer-generated image as your Web site's background to personalize your Web site. This causes some problems that can hinder your Web site's effectiveness. First, it makes the text on your Web site difficult to read. Second, it provides a distraction from what you want your Web site visitors to focus on — the images of your creative works and the text that describes the works and tells the visitors about your vision as an artist. Third, it makes your Web site pages load slowly, particularly for visitors who are using dial-up connections.

Instead of using a texture or an image as your background, stick to a plain-colored background that contrasts with the color of your text, so viewers can easily read the content of your Web site. A simple white, grey, or light blue background works well with black text; if you want to use a darker background, such as black or navy blue, use white text to tell viewers about your creative works. Also, make sure you use the same background and text colors for each page on your Web site — using different colors is distracting and shifts your visitors' focus away from the works you have displayed for sale.

Text

As you will see in the next chapter, text is as important as images for creating a Web site that attracts visitors. When designing your Web site, you should make sure the text is easy to find and read. As noted above, the color of your text should contrast with the color of your background. Colors look different on every computer monitor and laptop screen, so if you are having difficulty deciding between a background and text color combination that is aesthetically pleasing and one that balances well, choose the contrasting colors.

Avoid font sizes and styles that make your text difficult to read. A Web site with Old English text may be fun to create, but you can be sure few people will have the patience to read it.

Also, try to avoid multiple columns of text on a Web page. It is easier for the human eye to focus on a single column of text rather than multiple columns of text on a Web site. If you must use multiple columns, limit your Web pages to two columns. If you use any more than that, your Web site visitors will not have any focal point to visually anchor their eyes, and your Web page will seem jumbled and disorganized.

One exception to the one-column guideline is the sidebar. Sidebars are narrow vertical boxes, often with a background that is different from the rest of the Web site, that provide information you want to feature prominently on your site. This can include customer testimonials, links to works in progress, or any other information that may not be directly related to the content on your page but that is nevertheless important to your visitors.

Image Placement

If possible, your images should be centered horizontally on your Web pages between blocks of text. This creates a visual flow that will help your visitors stay focused on the content of your site.

Unless you are creating a gallery page, it is not a good idea to place two or three pictures along a horizontal line. This creates a sense of confusion on your Web page by providing too many items of equal prominence for your visitors to look at.

Images and Video

Although text is important for attracting and retaining Web site visitors, images are equally important, especially on an art-related Web site. People want to read about you and your creative works, but they also want to see Web sites filled with visually pleasing images. An art Web site without images will not retain your visitors for long — people expect the content of an art-related Web site to be more visually creative than business Web sites focusing on non-artistic fields, such as finance and banking.

In recent years, the Internet has experienced a shift in which Web site visitors have begun to expect more dynamic content. Because of this shift, dubbed Web 2.0 by Internet marketing professionals, more Web site owners are beginning to integrate video content into their Web pages.

Images and video help Web site visitors feel more connected to the content of the Web site and to the people involved in the business that the Web site promotes. For an artist, crafter, photographer, or musician, this is especially important. Purchasing artwork or music is an emotional decision, rather than a rational one, and visual media helps you connect to your visitors' emotions so they will feel the need to purchase your artworks rather than just admire them.

Images

Of course, you should include images of your artworks wherever possible, but you can also include images of things that inspire you — a hiking trail you walk to gather artistic ideas, a section of your city that gave you an idea for a series of creative works, or anything that ties into your career and vision as an artist.

As noted in the section on creating a biography page, you should include a professional head shot of yourself. You may also want to include other images of yourself, such as pictures of you working in your studio, standing next to one of your favorite artworks, or sitting in an environment that inspires you.

Some artists feel that including images of themselves takes the focus away from the artworks themselves, but including these images creates a sense of connection between you and your Web site visitors. People want to see the artistic genius behind the creative works, and having a few images of yourself on your Web site helps you tap into their curiosity.

Video

What video content can you include in your Web site to help generate visitor interest? Strangely, the content does not need to be a well-polished presentation of your work or a professional introduction to your career as an artist. You can set up an inexpensive video camera, or even a Web cam in your studio, and record yourself at work. Of course, you will not want your video to capture the voices of children playing in the background, but your video does not need to appear professionally produced. You may, however, want to use inexpensive video editing software to select and compile snippets of video from various stages of the creative process, so your visitors can see the creation of an artistic work from start to finish in a short time.

People who are not artistically inclined perceive the creation of art and music as a sort of magical process and have a natural inclination to want to see the creative process as it happens. This is why many DVDs released by major movie studios include behind-the-scenes footage of the making of the movie. Even if a moviegoer has already paid to see a movie in a theater, he or she may purchase the DVD just to see the behind-the-scenes footage.

You can use this curiosity to your advantage by including studio footage on your Web site. The video should be limited to two or three minutes in length, because you want your visitors to move on to other elements of your Web site, such as your gallery pages.

If you want to include video with a more professional appearance, you can record a short video introduction to your work without using professionals to record and edit your video. A short video of you in your studio, greeting your Web site visitors and inviting them to explore various areas of your site, will be sufficient to generate visitor interest.

You may want to watermark your images or add a copyright statement on each page to discourage visitors from downloading your images and using them on their own Web sites.

Site Maps

You should always include a site map somewhere in your Web site and provide a link to it on each page of your site. A site map is a document that shows every page and subpage of your Web site so that if your visitors are having difficulty finding what they are looking for on your site, they can refer to your site map to learn how to navigate to the information or products they are seeking.

Site maps are also helpful for search engines, because they provide a comprehensive list of pages and subpages on your site and provide links to each. This helps ensure that search engine spiders can find and index each page of your site so that you do not miss opportunities for visitors to find and visit your Web pages.

Google is beginning to require that large, complex Web sites include a site map before the site can be indexed. Google does not require site maps for smaller sites of ten or fewer pages, but it is a good idea to have one on your Web site to help visitors and search engine spiders find all your pages.

Many Web site creation programs offer a feature that will create a site map for you. If you are using a Web site creation tool that does not offer this feature, you can create a site map for free at **http:// google.com/webmasters/tools/docs/en/sitemap-generator.html.**

Now that you have learned about the elements that comprise a successful Web site, let us move on to techniques you can use to promote your Web site and generate traffic so you can begin making online sales. Chapter 4 will show you how to generate Web site, blog, and article content that will be useful for search engines while building the interest of your Web site visitors.

Content, Content, Content: Attracting Visitors to Your Web Site

You may think that, to create a successful Web site for selling your creative works, all you need are some images of your artworks, crafts, or photographs or some sample audio files of your music. After all, your creative works should be able to speak for themselves, right?

Although images and audio files are extremely important elements of any art business Web site, without text-based content, you will find your Web site wanting for visitors. Content is as equally important as images and audio to creating visitor interest for your business site and is absolutely crucial to driving traffic to your Web site. The words you put on your Web site are what will generate a constant stream of visitors that are looking for the creative works you have to offer.

This chapter covers the ways you can use content to make

your Web site visible. It is not a secret formula, but if you are not accustomed to creating Web site content for the purpose of generating traffic for your site, the process can be a little confusing. Fortunately, with a little direction and some practice, you can easily create content that will bring visitors to your Web site and keep them interested once they arrive.

Search Engines

The most common way people find a Web site out of the millions of sites occupying cyberspace is through a search engine, such as Google, MSN, or Yahoo!. The Introduction touched on the basics of a search engine query, but this section will delve into the details of how a search engine query works and how you can use your knowledge of this process to your advantage.

How Results are Selected after a Search Engine Query

In the Introduction, Web page numbers were obtained for several selected search terms — in almost every case, the search term produced more than 1,000,000 results on Google alone. Out of the millions of Web pages, ten were selected to appear on the first page of results listings. Who decides which Web pages will appear on the first page, and how?

Unless a Web site owner is content with having his or her site sit alone in cyberspace unvisited, the owner will submit a Web site to various search engines. Submitting a Web site just means the Web site owner has alerted the search engine that a new Web site exists or that it has been updated (you will find out how to do this in Chapter 7).

Once a Web site has been submitted to a search engine, the search engine will send spiders to the Web site to crawl for information. Spiders, of course, are not arachnids but rather a software program that scans the Web site for content. The spiders then report this information to the search engine's database, where the pages of a Web site are indexed and each page is ranked among the others for search terms.

A search engine's most basic goal in scanning each Web site for content is to determine how useful a Web site would be for an Internet user that types a particular query into a search engine box. The search engine's continued viability as a business depends on this because, if it continually produces irrelevant search results, users will simply move on to a different search engine.

The first page of search results is considered by the search engine to represent the Web pages that are the most relevant to what the search engine user is looking for. Getting your Web pages into these top ten results will garner substantially more traffic than having your Web pages on page four or after, because people rarely look at anything after the first two or three pages — either they have found what they are looking for, or they modify their search query to try to obtain more relevant results.

The actual method that search engines use to rank Web pages is proprietary, meaning the search engines do not make the methods, called algorithms, publicly available. This is because keeping the algorithms proprietary prevents competing search engines from copying the methods. Each search engine competes with all the others to provide the most relevant results for each query in an effort to get Internet users to use that search engine exclusively. To further complicate matters for Web site owners, the algorithm changes frequently — certain Web page elements may be made more or less important than others, which can change the rankings of results.

Although the algorithms used by the search engines to rank individual Web pages are kept secret, each search engine uses the same basic elements as criteria for ranking. This section outlines the elements considered for search engine placement and gives you tips on how to construct your Web pages to give you the best possible chance for your Web site to rank high in search results.

Keywords

Earlier in this book, you learned that Web site content is one of the most important elements of your Web pages. Here, you will learn why this is the case and how to write your content to be interesting for your Web site visitors and useful for search engine spiders.

The most important elements of your content are the keywords that appear within the content. Keywords are, at their most basic level, the terms an Internet user will type into a search engine query box to obtain Web page results. They include not only single words, but also phrases and common terms that a user would type in to search for Web pages.

Before you write a line of Web site content, you should sit down and take time to think like an Internet user who is trying to find the information, products, and services you provide on your Web site. This means focusing less on what you want to say and more on what your prospective visitors want to see.

Your Web site visitors are going to be specific about what they are looking for and will search using objective terms. If you were an Internet user looking for your particular products, what would you type into a search engine query box? Would you be more likely to type in "beautiful art" or "framed abstract art?" "Beautiful" is a subjective term, and your potential visitors know they are going to decide for themselves if a work of art, a photograph, or a piece of music is indeed beautiful. "Framed abstract art" is a search term that is much more likely to give them the results they are looking for.

In Chapter 8, you will learn how to determine how many other Web pages contain certain keywords and how likely these keywords are to be effective at improving your search engine rankings. For now, simply concentrate on thinking like a buyer instead of as a seller and compile a list of relevant, descriptive keywords to describe the products on your Web site.

For example, if you primarily paint abstract art on multiple canvases and use warm earth tones as your primary color palette, your initial list of keywords might look something like this:

⊛ Abstract art

- Abstract paintings

- Abstract art paintings

- Earth tone painting

- Earthtone painting

- Abstract earth tone painting

- Abstract earthtone painting

- Abstract art earth tones

- Abstract art earthtones

- Abstract art painting earth tones

- Abstract art painting earthtones

You could undoubtedly come up with many more keywords, but these are just a few that would accurately describe your works so that people searching for these terms would find your Web site relevant and stay on it to learn about and purchase your creative works.

Once you have compiled your initial list of relevant keywords, you are ready to begin building the content for your Web site.

Integrating Keywords into Your Site Content

The first place you will want to use your selected keywords to put your Web pages in a position to achieve high search engine rankings is in the content of your Web site itself. The home page of your Web site should be particularly rich in keywords, because that is the first page you will want visitors to find when they search for keywords that describe your products.

Using a particular keyword once on a Web page is not enough to obtain high search engine rankings for that page. Search engine spiders take into account not only whether a particular keyword appears on a page, but also how many times it appears in relation to the total number of words on the page. This ratio is called keyword density, and a Web page that has a high keyword density will rank better than a Web page that has a low density or a page where a keyword does not appear.

Internet marketers have different opinions about the correct keyword density for a Web page — that is, the density that is most likely to achieve an excellent search engine ranking for a page. Almost all these opinions will place the optimum keyword density somewhere between 1 and 4 percent for each keyword. If you construct your Web site content with a keyword density of 2 to 3 percent, you stand a good chance of having a Web page rank high in the search results for a particular keyword.

Obviously, it would be difficult to write Web site content that includes every single keyword two or three times for every 100 words. Your content would be completely unintelligible, and your Web site visitors would quickly move on to another site. It is best to select one primary keyword for each Web page and one or two secondary keywords that are included at a lower keyword density.

Placement of keywords is also an important factor in obtaining high search engine rankings. Your primary keyword should appear in the first sentence of the first paragraph on the page and preferably within the first four words, if possible. It should also appear in the second paragraph and at least once in the last paragraph on the page.

Using this ratio, your Web site content should include a keyword at least twice for every 100 words on a Web page. Using the example from the previous section, here is what a section of the content for your home page may look like. The keywords are shown in bold:

Choosing **abstract art paintings** for your home or office can be a difficult task, especially if you are shopping for **abstract art** online. This can be especially hard if you are looking for **earth tone paintings** — the colors in these artworks show up a bit differently on each computer monitor, so matching the colors to your décor can be a challenge.

When you purchase your **abstract art paintings** from my studio, you will not have to worry about whether the colors of your **earth tone paintings** blend with your décor. I have painstakingly photographed each artwork to ensure the colors are represented accurately on your computer screen, so you can be sure the colors you see are as true as possible. Although it takes a little more time and effort to photograph my **abstract art paintings** this way, the additional effort has resulted in many happy customers who are delighted that the paintings look just like the images on my Web site.

If, for some reason, you purchase one of my **abstract art paintings** that just does not match the colors of your home or office, just contact me, and I will be happy to refund your money and give you instructions for shipping the painting back to me.

This short section consists of 209 words. The keyword "abstract art paintings" appears four times in this section, giving the content a density of about 2 percent for that keyword. The secondary keyword, "earth tone paintings," appears twice, giving it a keyword density of about 1 percent. The secondary keyword, "abstract art," appears only once but can be used again in other sections of the Web page's content to improve keyword density.

Readable, Useful, Keyword-Optimized Content

The challenge for many Web site content writers is to create Web site copy that contains the correct density of keywords while making the content interesting and useful for the readers. Having a Web page that is perfectly optimized will not help you make sales if the content is not interesting to your Web site visitors.

To create Web site content that is both interesting and engaging for your readers and useful for search engine spiders, start by writing your Web site content as if you were writing a letter to a friend. Use easy-to-read, conversational language that your visitors can relate to. Avoid using big or obscure words — it is tempting to use Web site content to showcase your vocabulary, but if your copy contains too many words that your readers need a dictionary to understand, they will quickly lose interest and move on to another Web site.

Also, use descriptive language in your copy — do not simply assume the images on your site will speak for themselves. Although well-photographed, brilliant images are imperative to creating a successful art Web site, your readers need descriptive content to fully appreciate how incredible your artworks or crafts will look in their homes or how energizing your music will sound when they are listening to it on the way to work or school.

Another way to create engaging Web site content is through the use of stories. People love to hear stories, and if you can tell a story in your Web site copy, you can be sure your visitors will more closely connect with your creative works. This makes them more likely to want to purchase one of your works for themselves.

Your first draft of the home page copy may look something like this:

> Hello and thank you for stopping by my Web site. My name is Joe Smith, and I have been photographing the landscape of the American Southwest for nearly 20 years. I am in awe of the majestic scenery of the desert — the jutted cliffs and winding canyons have

inspired me since the first time my father and I ambled through the Arizona desert in a well-worn Jeep, stopping every now and again to admire the colors and shapes of the rock formations.

I was seven years old on that first trip, and my dad's manual 35mm camera became my means of immortalizing our time together. It also created my lifelong love of photography — since that day, I have made countless journeys through the desert, camera bag in tow, searching for new compositions that capture the freedom and spirit of the American Southwest.

My father passed away a few years ago, but his voice is alive and well when I am wandering through the desert, capturing images of fiery sunsets spilling swaths of pink and orange across the rolling sand. Most of my photographs are still taken with that old manual camera that fueled my love of photography so many years ago.

Please feel free to browse my gallery page to see the Southwest photographs I have collected over the years. I hope you enjoy the composition and color of these desert images as much as I have enjoyed creating them. Perhaps you will even find an image that speaks to you and allows you to connect with the majesty of the American Southwest. If so, I would be honored to have such a photograph hanging in your home or office.

Let us examine this short example, to determine why it resonates with the reader:

- It uses simple, conversational language. It addresses the reader and reads as if the Web site visitor is a close friend, instead of a prospective buyer.

- It uses descriptive words to help the reader visualize the images in the photographs. It describes winding canyons, fiery sunsets, and jutted cliffs — phrases that make the reader feel as if he or she was in the Jeep with the writer, looking out at the desert landscape.

- It tells a story. The Web site visitor learns about the writer's first experience with photography and relates the writer's photographic career to his relationship with his father. The reader will likely think of his or her own experiences exploring new territory with a parent, which creates a perceived connection between the reader and the artist.

After you have written the first draft of your Web site content, look at the keywords you have chosen for your Web site. You may find these keywords already appear in your copy. Now, you will simply need to look for ways you can integrate additional uses of the keywords to optimize your Web site content for search engines.

Let us consider the example copy. Suppose the artist wants to concentrate on the keywords "desert images" and "Southwest photographs" on the home page. Both keywords appear only once in the example copy and only near the end of the content. Since the content is 280 words long, each keyword has a density of only 0.3 percent — not nearly enough to be useful for search engine spiders.

The example content could be easily revised to increase the keyword density. Here is how the revised copy may look (changes are shown in bold):

Hello and thank you for stopping by my Web site **to see my Southwest photographs and desert images**. My name is Joe Smith, and I have been photographing the landscape of the American Southwest for nearly 20 years. I am in awe of the majestic scenery of the desert — the jutted cliffs and winding canyons have inspired me **to create desert images** since the first time my father and I ambled through the Arizona desert in a well-worn Jeep, stopping every now and again to admire the colors and shapes of the rock formations.

I was seven years old on that first trip, and my dad's manual 35mm camera became my means of immortalizing our time together. It also created my lifelong love of **taking Southwest photographs** — since that day, I have made countless journeys through the desert, camera bag in tow, searching for new compositions that capture the freedom and spirit of the American Southwest **through my desert images**.

My father passed away a few years ago, but his voice is alive and well when I am wandering through the desert, capturing images of fiery sunsets spilling swaths of pink and orange across the rolling sand. Most of my **Southwest** photographs are still taken with that old manual camera that fueled my love of photography so many years ago.

Please feel free to browse my gallery page to see the Southwest photographs **and desert images** I have collected over the years. I hope you enjoy the composition and color of these desert images as much as I have enjoyed creating them. Perhaps you will even find an image that speaks to you and allows you to connect with the majesty of the American Southwest. If so, I would be honored to have such a photograph hanging in your home or office.

With the addition of just a few words, the revised example achieves a density of 1.64 percent for the keyword "desert images," and a density of 1.31 percent for the keyword "Southwest photographs." The additional keywords flow seamlessly into the content, and it will not be obvious to the reader that your copy concentrates on the keywords.

Building readable content around keywords takes a bit of practice, but once you have changed your writing mind-set to pay attention to keyword density, it becomes a relatively easy task.

Using Keywords in Title Tags

The software or Web application you will use for your Web site will require that you choose a title for each Web page — if you are using Internet Explorer, this title will appear in the blue bar at the top of the page when it is viewed online.

If you do not specify a title tag, your Web site creation tool will assign a generic tag to each page — "Home," "Page 2," "Page 3," and so on. Although this may not seem like a big problem, settling on default page titles robs you of a chance to improve your page search rankings.

Instead of letting your page titles become your Web site creation tool's default settings, craft your page titles around the primary keywords for each page. Going back to the abstract art Web site example, an appropriate title tag would be "Abstract Art Paintings by Joe Smith." You can even incorporate a secondary keyword into your page title, as long as the title is ten or fewer words. "Abstract Art Paintings — Earth Tone Paintings by Joe Smith" would be a good page title that conveys the purpose of the Web page to your visitors and includes two keywords for search engine placement purposes.

Web Page Description

Your Web site creation tool will also allow you to provide a description for each Web page. This description will not appear on the Web page itself but will appear in the search engine listing under the page title.

This description will give Internet users browsing search engine listings a little more information about what is contained on that page. It should be easily readable and should give your potential visitors a brief overview of what they can expect to find if they click on your link in the search engine listings.

It is also another good opportunity to use your primary and

secondary keywords to improve your Web page's ranking for those keywords. Spiders will use text contained in these descriptions as a factor in determining where your Web page will rank in relation to other Web pages targeting these keywords.

Using the abstract art example again, here is an example of a Web page description (including the title) that will inform your readers and improve your search engine rankings:

Abstract Art Paintings — Earth Tone Paintings by Joe Smith

Joe Smith Studio Online features abstract art paintings that are perfect for the home or office. Browse abstract art and earth tone paintings for every budget. Shipping included on abstract art purchases over $200.

This Web page description leaves little room for ambiguity — your visitors will know what to expect when they click on the link to visit your Web site. It also contains your primary keyword and both secondary keywords for your page. It also lets your visitors know you offer a purchase incentive in the form of complimentary shipping for orders more than $200.

Notice that the Web page description contained the words "shipping included" rather than "free shipping." This is because the word "free" is viewed negatively by the search engine spiders — partially because it is used by so many millions of Web pages that it is deemed irrelevant and partially because the word "free" is associated with scam Web sites that owners use to collect information so they can spam users or inundate them with unwanted e-mails and pop up messages. For these reasons, it is a good idea to avoid using the word "free" anywhere in your Web site's content, even if you are offering something that is indeed free.

Meta Tags

Another element you can include in your Web pages to improve your search engine rankings is the meta tag. Meta tags are words or phrases that are inserted into the header section of the HTML code of your Web page — the part of the code that tells the browser certain information about the Web page that human visitors need not be concerned with.

Your Web site visitors will not see the meta tags you use for each Web page, but search engine spiders will see them. You can use your keywords in the meta tag field to tell the search engine spiders about the contents of your Web page, above and beyond the information available in your page content.

If you looked at the HTML header code for the home page of the abstract art Web site, here is what it might look like:

<HEAD>

<TITLE>Abstract Art Paintings — Earth Tone Paintings by Joe Smith</TITLE>

<META Name="description" content="Joe Smith Studio Online

features abstract art paintings that are perfect for the home or office. Browse abstract art and earth tone paintings for every budget. Shipping included on abstract art purchases over $200.">

<META Name="keywords" content="abstract art, abstract art paintings, earth tone painting, earth tone painting">

</HEAD>

Some Internet marketers argue that meta tags are no longer important for improving your search engine rankings and that search engine spiders no longer use meta tags when compiling rankings. Given that the algorithms used by search engines are proprietary, it is impossible to tell which search engines use meta tags as criteria for ranking Web pages.

Since it is not possible to determine whether meta tags are used by a particular search engine, the small amount of time you will spend creating tags for your pages will be, at worst, a way to easily remember which keywords you targeted for each Web page and, at best, another way to bolster your Web site content to help your pages achieve better rankings.

Image Tags

An often overlooked technique for using keywords to improve your Web site's search engine rankings is to place relevant keywords in your image tags, also called ALT tags.

If you have ever browsed a Web site and held the pointer over an image and a small yellow box appeared with a short description of the image, you may have wondered why the Web site owner bothered to do this. After all, is not the content of the image self-explanatory?

Although you can look at an image and tell right away what is contained in the image, search engine spiders do not have this ability. The spiders know an image exists, but they cannot derive any useful information from it. The ALT tag is a way to describe the image to the search engine spider. It is also a useful tool for loading your Web pages with a few additional keywords.

Your ALT tags should be short — no more than eight to ten words — and should contain no more than one or two keywords. They should also accurately describe the image with words that are as specific as possible to the image's content.

An example of an ALT tag for an abstract artwork called "Geometric Landscape" may look something like this:

Geometric Landscape — Abstract Art Paintings series — Earth Tones Painting

This ALT tag gives Web site visitors the name of the painting and includes the primary keyword and one of the secondary keywords targeted for that page.

Techniques to Avoid When Using Keywords in Your Web Site Content

All the techniques described above for including keywords in your Web site's content are considered ethical and valid. In Internet marketing circles, they are known as "White Hat" techniques, referring to the old Western movies in which the good guys wore white hats.

Over the years, though, Web site owners have used a number of other techniques to try to gain additional advantages for search engine ranking purposes. Search engines are aware of all these techniques and have programmed spiders to detect the use of unethical techniques, known in the Internet marketing community as "Black Hat" techniques (uses of keywords that are clearly unethical) or "Grey Hat" techniques (uses of keywords that are highly questionable).

Not only will the use of unethical or questionable techniques fail to improve your Web site's search engine rankings, it can cause search engines to permanently ban your Web site altogether. This means that, even if you correct the problem, you will never be able to have your Web site ranked on that search engine. If your Web site gets banned on a small or regional search engine, it is bad news for your marketing efforts; if it gets banned on a major search engine such as Google or MSN Search, the consequences will be downright disastrous.

Here is a list of keyword techniques that will get your Web site banned on nearly any search engine.

Keyword Stuffing

Earlier in this chapter, you learned about keyword density — using keywords in a certain ratio to the total number of words on a Web page to improve your search engine rankings. As noted earlier, a keyword density of between 1 and 4 percent is considered useful for building rankings.

Some Web site owners reason that if 4 percent is good, then 10 percent or more must be fantastic. Unfortunately, using keywords excessively constitutes a technique known as keyword stuffing — using a keyword so many times in a Web page's contents that the text cannot possibly be useful to Web site visitors.

Keyword stuffing is fairly easy to spot, even for people that are new to the Internet. Read the following example of Web site content that uses keyword stuffing in an effort to gain a better search engine ranking for a Web page:

Do you like abstract art paintings? Then check out my abstract art paintings. These abstract art paintings are done in earth tones and are some of the best abstract art paintings you will find on the Internet today. You can find abstract art paintings on a number of Web sites, but those abstract art paintings are not anything like the abstract art paintings you will find on this Web site, which is full of abstract art paintings you will love. Whether you are looking for abstract art paintings for your home or abstract art paintings for your office, you will be sure to find abstract art paintings that will be perfect for your décor.

I am adding new abstract art paintings every day, so even if the abstract art paintings you find here are not what you are looking for, check back often for new abstract art paintings — chances are, you will find new abstract art paintings soon that will perfectly meet your need for abstract art paintings.

This short, 168-word passage uses the keyword "abstract art paintings" 16 times — that is a keyword density ratio of 10.5 percent. For the human visitor, it amounts to a ridiculous passage that has little value and is rather irritating to read. For a search engine spider, it amounts to keyword stuffing, and a Web page containing this passage would stand little chance of ever being ranked in a search engine's listings.

Aside from using the acceptable ratio of 1 to 4 percent for keyword density, another good rule of thumb that can be used is far less mathematical and far more intuitive. If you or a friend reads a passage and picks up on the fact that a certain keyword is being heavily targeted, you may be overusing the keyword in that passage. Even if your Web page does not get banned for keyword stuffing, the overuse of search terms is likely to irritate your Web site visitors and send them looking for products elsewhere.

Invisible Text

Invisible text is an old favorite for those who use Black Hat techniques. Invisible text has been used on Web sites for several years in an effort to improve Web pages' search engine rankings. This technique uses elements of keyword stuffing (albeit at keyword density ratios that are much higher than those used for visible text), but users of this technique try to hide its use by making the text color the same as the background color, so human visitors will not be able to see it. The hidden text is placed at the bottom of a Web page, where visitors are not likely to notice a section of seemingly blank space.

The hidden text consists almost entirely of keywords without any regard for useful comments or principals of good grammar. If you scrolled down to a blank space at the bottom of a Web page on which this technique is employed, clicked, held the left mouse button, and dragged the mouse across the blank space, you might highlight a block of text that looks something like this:

Abstract art paintings abstract art earthtone paintings abstract art paintings earth tone paintings abstract earth tone paintings abstract art earth tone paintings earthtone paintings abstract art abstract earthtone paintings abstract art paintings abstract art earthtones abstract art earthtones abstract art abstract art paintings

Although most visitors will not pick up on this use of hidden keyword stuffing because they are shopping for art and not trying to find Web sites with unethical keyword usage, search engine spiders will pick up on this technique. Not only that, but they will recognize this as an attempt to cheat the ranking system and then ban the Web site from search engine listings.

It can be tempting to use this technique, reasoning that, since the search engine spiders cannot tell what is contained in an image, they cannot tell what color the text is in relation to the Web site's background either. Since this technique has become so popular, however, search engines have programmed spiders to not only pick up on text and background colors that are the same, but also color combinations that are similar. Thus, using a light pink text on a white background will garner no better results than using white on white.

You will gain nothing by using this strategy and run the risk of permanently losing the ability to have your Web site appear in search engine listings.

Doorway Pages

This is another technique commonly used by Web site owners to try to cheat their way to better rankings. A doorway page is a Web page that is never seen by human visitors because, as soon as a visitor lands on that page by clicking on a search engine listing, the visitor is redirected to another page on the Web site.

The content on the doorway page is laden with keywords — in essence, an entire page of text similar to that used in the invisible text example above. The theory is that the search engine spiders will read and index the content from this page, and the content's high keyword density will cause the Web site to be ranked higher in the search engine listings.

This is not an effective technique because search engine spiders are programmed to recognize a doorway page by the redirect instructions written into the page's code. Although there are some other legitimate uses for doorway pages that are outside the scope of this book, the combination of a redirect command and heavy keyword density will cause your doorway page to be marked as a Black Hat technique. Then, you will never have to worry about how to improve your Web site's ranking again, because it will never appear in the search engine listings.

Blogging

Blogging is another important tool for gaining Web site visibility, because it exposes your Web site to people searching for your products via a search engine and to people just searching for quality content to read as they are surfing the Internet. You can attract hundreds or thousands of visitors to your Web site just by writing about various aspects of your art, your business, and your opinions about various aspects of your creative field.

Blogging means creating an online diary to which you add content on a regular basis. Each entry in a blog is referred to as a post, which is stamped with the date and time you submitted the entry online for the entire world to see. The posts in a blog can be arranged in chronological order (oldest to newest), reverse chronological order (newest to oldest), or by topic.

There are two primary methods you can use to build a blog that will improve your Web site traffic. The first is to include a blog as a page, or series of pages, on your Web site. This will give your Web site visitors another reason to keep coming back to your Web site for new content, and it will give you yet another chance to use keywords to help improve your Web site's search engine rankings.

The second is to keep a blog on one of the many popular blogging sites, such as **www.blogger.com**, **www.xanga.com**, or **wordpress. com**. Although starting and maintaining a blog on one of these sites will not allow you to use keywords to directly affect your Web site's rankings, it will allow visitors to the blogging site to discover and learn about your creative works, which will compel them to visit your main Web site to obtain more information or to purchase one of your works.

You may even choose to keep more than one blog — one on your main Web site and one or more on other sites. This gives you the best of both worlds, because it allows you to improve your own Web site's content while reaching people outside search engine queries. If you do this, it is a good idea to make sure the content on each of these blogs is at least somewhat different — search engine spiders crawl Web sites and blogs, and duplicate content may cause both to be penalized.

With an estimated 70 million blogs on the Internet today, getting people to read your blog takes a little more than just writing about your career. There are several techniques you can use to make your blog visible so that it can become a useful tool for your business.

Join Blogrings

On most blogging sites, blogs are divided into categories and subcategories according to the main theme or topic of each blog. Blogrings are groups of blogs that share a common theme, interest, or predominant topic.

In the world of the creative arts, you will find blogring categories pertaining to visual and fine arts, crafts, photography, and music, among many others. From there, you will find numerous subcategories — painting, sculpture, wicker crafts, wood carvings, landscape photography, rock music, and ambient music; the list goes on.

When you join a blogring dedicated to your particular niche in the creative arts, you will not only find other working artists with similar objectives, but you will also find their customers. An Internet user that regularly reads a blog written by a fellow artist offering similar products will also be interested in reading your blog and visiting your Web site to see what you have to offer.

Blogrings are also wonderful tools for networking with other working artists. By staying in contact with fellow members of an art-related blogring, you can find out about new trends in the online marketplace, contests for creative artists, new places to find discounted supplies and services, and new opportunities to get your creative works in front of the buying public. Working artists understand the challenge of making a living online, and blogrings present an opportunity to connect with these artists, learn from their experiences, and benefit from their connections.

Use Blog Compilation Web Sites

Another way to gain visibility for your blog (and thus for your Web site) is to make sure your blog posts appear on blog compilation services like **www.technorati.com**. These compilation services collect information about new blog posts from thousands of Web sites every hour and compile them in a way that makes it easy for visitors to find posts on any topic imaginable.

These compilation services also allow visitors to subscribe to specific blogs and feature blog posts on their own Web sites. This is done via RSS feeds, which are programs that allow content from one Web site to automatically appear on another Web site without the RSS feed subscriber having to manually update his or her Web site to feature the new content.

This works out well for the Web site owner subscribing to the RSS feed, because he or she has the benefit of constantly having fresh content on his or her Web site without having to write new content or spend time uploading it to the Web site. It also works out well for you, because you gain an instant audience, consisting of everyone who regularly visits the subscribing member's Web site.

Provide Informative, Conversational Content

One of the best ways to ensure that your blog will be read is to frequently update it with content that is fresh, informative, and written in an informal, conversational style. Internet users crave new information, and if you can provide relevant information that makes the reader feel more like he or she is having a conversation with a good friend and less like he or she is reading an essay, you will find that people come back to read your blog regularly.

As a creative businessperson, what types of things should you blog about? You can easily use a blog to show the progress of an artwork or song you have been working on. This is a way to build a readership base that comes back day after day for new content, because they will want to check in to see how the new creative work is coming along. Do not be afraid to include images or even video to build interest while you are documenting the progress of your latest creative endeavor. Blogging Web sites make this quite easy to do, and it will help you attract and retain readers. The pictures and video will make your readers feel even more like they are part of something special, something unique, and something that not everyone is taking part in.

You can also write about artworks you plan on creating soon, art shows and contests you have attended, upcoming exhibits featuring fellow artists, and even your personal life, if you are comfortable doing so. Your blog posts should bear at least some relevance to your business, but you have quite a bit more latitude to include personal information and opinions than you do on the main pages of your Web site.

Do not forget to include information about sales, specials such as free shipping, or other promotions you are currently running on your Web site. You can use your blog to create a sense of urgency so that your readers will click on the link to your Web site right away to take advantage of whatever incentives you are currently offering.

It is also important that you update your blog frequently — if you post less than once a week, readers are likely to forget to come back for new content. It can be difficult to find time to write a blog post every day while you are busy creating your artworks, crafts, photography, or music, but you should set aside some time to post at least three to four times per week.

Article Writing and Submission

A third way to use content to drive traffic to your Web site is by writing articles and submitting them to article directories. As noted earlier in this chapter, Web sites rely on content for search engine rankings, and many Web site owners use content taken from article directories to provide fresh copy for search engine spiders to use to rank their sites.

By writing articles and submitting them to directories, you can provide content for other Web site owners to use. The better the quality of your content, the more often Web site owners will use your articles for their own sites.

Why would you want to write content for other people's Web sites? First, it establishes you as an expert in your business — by providing content to article directories that is informative and useful, you give Internet surfers the opportunity to see how much you know about your particular type of art, crafts, photography, or music.

Second, it helps your Web site gain exposure and traffic. When a Web site owner chooses to use one of your articles to build content for a Web site, he or she will be required to include your biographical information. This is a short paragraph at the end of your articles that tells the reader a little about you and provides a link to your Web site. Having this biographical information on another site not only provides readers with a way to see your creative works, but it also helps your Web site gain a better search engine ranking via the one-way link included in your bio (more on link building in Chapter 5).

Third, article marketing helps to build branding on the Internet. The more articles you write and submit to article directories, the more widely known your business will become. If you write articles that resonate with readers and have memorable content that readers can put to practical use, people will remember your business the next time they need an artwork for a home or office, photographs for a Web site, or new music for a trip.

These benefits make article marketing worth your time because, over a period of several months, article marketing will generate substantially more business than if you relied on search engine marketing and blogging alone.

Deciding What to Write About

Articles that you write for article directories should somehow relate to your business — if you are a fine artist, your articles should relate to painting, sculpture, or whatever style of art you create. If you are a photographer, your articles should relate to some aspect of photography.

Your articles should contain practical information that readers can directly apply to their own endeavors. For example, if you are a painter, your articles could be about some aspect of selecting, displaying, or creating two-dimensional artworks. Here are some examples of topics that a painter might use for articles:

- How to correctly hang and display artworks in a home or office

- How to provide optimal lighting to make an artwork stand out in a room

- How to choose a painting that complements a room's style and décor

- How to select colors for creating a painting

- Techniques for creating realistic effects with oil paints

Your articles are not about selling your works, but rather about establishing yourself as an authority as a creative person and providing information readers can readily use in their own lives. If you focus on promoting and selling your creative works in your article content, your articles will not be widely distributed and will not help your Web site obtain a better search engine ranking or gain more traffic.

Submitting Your Articles to Article Directories

Once you have written several articles relating to your art business, you will want to begin submitting them to article directories so they can begin generating exposure for your Web site.

Signing up for a membership to an article directory is easy — just fill in your contact information and give a brief description of the types of articles you write, and you will be ready to start submitting articles for online publication and distribution.

There are hundreds of article directories available on the Internet that you can use to promote your Web site. Some of the better-known article directories include **www.ezinearticles.com, www.articledashboard.com,** and **www.goarticles.com.** A quick Google search will turn up plenty of other Web sites you can use to publish your articles.

Nearly all the article directories have the same basic format for submitting your articles. You will fill in several fields with information about your article and then submit it to the directory for review and publication. Since most article directories share a similar format, you can write your article and supporting information once via Microsoft Word or another word processing tool and quickly upload your article to multiple directories.

Here are the elements required by most article directories:

- ⊛ **Your Name.** This is the name that will appear as the author of the article. You can choose to use either your own name, or the name of your business (Joe Smith Art Studio).

- ⊛ **Your Article Category.** Most submission pages have a drop-down menu for this field, allowing you to scroll through all the available categories to choose the one that most closely fits the subject of your article.

Choosing an article category that closely relates to the content of your article will help your article gain greater exposure. Just as search engine users expect accurate results, Web site owners that use articles for online content expect to find articles that accurately reflect the category they are searching under.

If you are a painter, you may choose Arts and Humanities: Fine Art as your article category. If you are a musician, Arts and Humanities: Music may be a good choice.

- ⊛ **Keywords.** Web site owners looking for content articles can also search for keywords to find articles that will mesh well with the purpose of their sites. Choose keywords that accurately reflect the content of your article. For example, if you write an article on how to correctly hang a painting in a home or office, your keyword choices may look like this:

Hanging painting, display painting, framing painting, hang painting, correct painting height, how to hang a painting

Choosing accurate keywords will give your article the best chance of being published on multiple Web sites and will help ensure your articles are published on Web sites that are visited by people who will be interested in your creative works.

- ⊛ **Article Summary.** This is a brief description of your article that Web site owners will see when they search for articles to use as content. Your article summary should be written to entice article directory users to read the full article and use it on their Web sites.

Here is an example of an article summary that will make Web site owners want to read your article:

Have you ever wondered how to display a painting in your home or office so that it will perfectly complete the décor of your room? This article gives you step-by-step instructions on how to choose a location for your painting, how to select the correct height for your artwork, and how to set up your lighting so your painting becomes an elegant conversation piece for any room.

This example description does not just tell what the article is about; it shows the reader how your article can help solve a common problem.

- **Article Body.** This is the actual article you have written for publication. You should be able to simply cut and paste your article from your word processor.

- **Author Bio.** Web site owners that use your articles must include your biography after the article text. You can use this biography to highlight your talents and experience and provide a link to the Web site on which you sell your creative works.

Here is an example of an author bio that will generate traffic for your Web site:

Joe Smith has been creating abstract paintings for more than 15 years and currently serves as the gallery design consultant for the Buckeye Art Gallery in Columbus, Ohio. To see Joe's artworks or request a commissioned painting, please visit www.joesmithartgallery.com.

Affiliate Marketing

Affiliate marketing can be another good technique for driving traffic to your Web site and generating sales of your creative works. Using affiliate marketing involves enlisting other Internet marketers to generate interest for your Web site and sending visitors to you so they can view and purchase your artworks, crafts, photographs, or music.

In exchange for driving traffic to your Web site, affiliate marketers expect to receive a percentage of the sales that result from the traffic they send. The percentage varies according to the type of product you are selling — for physical products such as artworks or crafts, you can offer a commission of 10 to 20 percent; for intangible products, such as digital photographic images or music downloads, you may need to offer a commission of 50 percent or more to attract affiliate marketers that will aggressively market your products.

To attract talented affiliate marketers, you may also want to offer a percentage of future sales made to repeat buyers — this percentage can be lower than the commission for the initial sale, but it will still represent an opportunity for residual commissions and will encourage your affiliates to work harder to promote your products.

Some Web site owners that market their products through affiliates choose to manage their own affiliate marketing programs, calculating the commissions of their affiliates and paying them via check or PayPal.

Other Web site owners prefer to outsource their affiliate management tasks to a third party Web site, such as Commission Junction or ClickBank. These Web sites list affiliate marketing opportunities and handle the calculation and payment of commissions from sales derived from affiliate marketers' efforts.

These Web sites also charge Web site owners for listing an affiliate marketing opportunity — the fee is less than $50 per listing. They may also charge the Web site owner a portion of commissions paid as compensation for calculating and managing affiliate commissions. These Web sites usually do not charge fees to the marketers that are promoting your products.

You can list your affiliate opportunity on **www.clickbank.com, www.cj.com, www.linkshare.com,** and a variety of other Web sites. Before listing your opportunity on one of these Web sites, take time to explore the site to make sure the format of the site and the types of products offered by Web site owners are compatible with your products — your creative works.

If you choose to offer an affiliate program to help build your online sales, it is a good idea to create a page on your Web site to explain your opportunity to potential affiliate marketers. You will need to explain who your target market is, tell what other kinds of marketing strategies you are using, and give your potential affiliates tips and suggestions for marketing your products. After all, you know your creative works far better than your affiliate marketers, so they will look to you for direction on how to effectively promote your works.

You should also give your affiliate marketers several advertisements they can use in their Web sites, blogs, and articles, along with the HTML code necessary to insert the advertisements. These advertisements could include graphics that link to your Web site and text links that point to your site or a gallery page within your site.

Your advertisements should contain short messages that will entice visitors to click on the links to visit your Web site. For example, you could create an advertisement with a message such as, "White walls? Bring them alive with art! www. joesmithartstudio.com."

You can also integrate affiliate marketing with article marketing by creating and publishing articles that encourage affiliate marketers to sign up for your program. These articles should highlight some aspect of using art to improve the décor of a home or office or focus on another topic that deals with using creative works to provide enjoyment to buyers, rather than focusing on a technical aspect of art, crafting, photography, or music creation.

Although your profit percentage will be lower for creative works sold through affiliate marketers than for works sold to people who visit your Web site directly, you can save a significant amount of time and money by using affiliate marketing to promote your works. This is because your affiliates are responsible for promoting your products and will bear the costs of marketing.

Affiliate marketing represents an arrangement that is beneficial to both you and your affiliates. You have the opportunity to experience an increase in sales without expending additional resources for marketing, and your affiliates have the opportunity to make money through online sales without having to create their own products.

You will probably not want to depend solely on affiliates to market your products, but if you want to build your business quickly with minimal advertising costs, affiliate marketing can be an effective way to build an online fan base without spending countless hours creating marketing copy and promoting your Web site.

Squidoo

Creating an account on Squidoo is another effective technique for generating interest for your creative works and driving traffic to your Web site. Squidoo is a Web site that allows users to create pages, called lenses, about specific topics and build biographies that invite readers to visit the owner's Web site for more information.

To create a Squidoo account, visit **www.squidoo.com** and click on the Sign Up link at the top of the page. You will enter your name, desired username, password, and e-mail address, and your account will be created within minutes.

Once you have created your Squidoo account, you can create as many lenses as you like. Each of your lenses should contain informational content that will be of interest to your potential customers. Lenses are not primarily for directly promoting your Web site or your creative works but for giving Squidoo users information that helps establish you as an authority in your artistic field so visitors will want to know more about you and the artworks or music you create.

Although the main focus of a Squidoo lens should be informational content, you can include a number of other elements, called modules, that will help promote your art business.

RSS Feeds

An easy way to generate additional interest for your creative works is to include an RSS feed of your art-related blog. An RSS feed automatically places the content of your blog into your Squidoo lens and updates every time you add a new post to your blog. This is a good way to keep people coming back to your lens, because they know your lens will always contain fresh content.

To create an RSS feed on your Squidoo lens, click on the RSS feed module on your editing page and enter the URL of your blog. Squidoo will pull content from your blog and display it on your lens page.

eBay Auctions

If you sell some of your creative works on eBay, you can include a module that contains all your current auction listings. This is a way to introduce people to your work and build long-term customer relationships because people can easily find and bid on your creative works in the hopes of obtaining a work at a discounted price.

In your lens editing page, click the Add a Module button and select an eBay module from the next page. This will add an eBay module to your lens. Then, select the Edit button on your new eBay module to add auction listings.

You will have the choice of allowing Squidoo to select auctions based on your keywords or tags, or you can select auctions yourself. If you choose to select auction listings yourself, you can either select individual auctions or have Squidoo list all the auctions listed under your username.

Link List

You can use this module to provide links to your Web site, your blog, articles you have published in article directories, or any other sites or pages that provide additional information to help you build customer interest and generate sales. Not only will your link list give you additional opportunities to draw in potential buyers, it will also help raise the search engine rankings of all the sites and pages you link to. You will learn more about using links to improve Web site visibility in Chapter 5.

Guestbook

You can add a guestbook to your Squidoo lens so visitors to your lens can leave comments about you or your content. As your lens increases in popularity, you will build a guestbook that lets visitors know that people enjoy your artwork and other content. Much like testimonials on your Web site, this helps you tap into the herd mentality — people will automatically be more receptive to your creative works because other people have already expressed public approval of your work.

There are a number of other modules you can add to your Squidoo lens to generate visitor interest and help drive traffic to your Web site. One of the most important elements, though, is the text module, where you can add articles and other information to gain exposure for your Squidoo lens and familiarize visitors with your particular style of creative work.

You can also use modules to earn extra money — for example, you can add an Amazon module that features books and other products on **www.amazon.com** that are relevant to your lens and your main Web site. Squidoo will pay you 50 percent of the affiliate commissions derived from sales on Amazon that result from your Squidoo links. Be careful not to use too many of these, because any modules that link to other Web sites you do not own can rob your Web site of traffic. You want as many people as possible who visit your lens to follow links to your Web site, blog, and articles so they will be more likely to purchase creative works from you.

Now that you have learned about the many ways you can use online content to promote your creative works and drive traffic to your site, let us move on to another way you can improve your Web site's search engine rankings and attract more customers to your site: link building.

Link Building

Aside from engaging, keyword-optimized content, one of the most important elements for gaining Web site visibility is link building. You have probably noticed that, on almost all Web sites, there are sections of underlined text that will take you to other pages on the Web site or to different Web sites altogether. These sections of text are called hyperlinks, or links for short.

Web site owners use links to help visitors find their way around a Web site or find different Web sites that are useful. They also use links in testimonials to help provide credibility for the comments made in the testimonials — visitors can click on links to sites owned by the people giving accolades to the Web site owner to help establish that they are real people.

Links are also used by search engines as yet another criterion to determine where a Web page should rank in relation to all the other Web pages using the same keywords.

To understand how search engines use links to help determine where a Web page should be ranked in the search engine listings, think of the friends-by-association phenomenon you probably encountered in high school. Although a certain amount of your popularity was determined by your own personal characteristics, such as looks, personality, and interests, a substantial amount of your popularity was also determined by the friends you chose and the people who accepted you into their groups or cliques. If you were friends with the captain of the football team, that association gained you quite a bit more popularity than if you were friends with the captain of the chess team. In turn, being friends with the chess team captain carried substantially more weight than if you were friends with the students who skipped classes to smoke in the parking lot. Finally, although associating with the class skippers was not an enviable position, at least in terms of popularity, it carried more weight than not having any friends.

Link building works in much the same way. Having a well-established, high-ranking Web site link to yours will carry substantial weight in determining the search engine rankings for your own Web site. A link to your Web site from a moderately traveled Web site with mediocre search engine rankings will still help you improve your search engine rankings, but not as much as if you had an inbound link from a Web site that consistently appeared in the top ten rankings. Getting a link from your friend's Web site on 12th century European farming techniques may not make much of a difference, but it is still better than having no inbound links.

In addition to the quality of the links your Web site receives, search engines also consider the number of inbound links. Having 50 links from moderately successful Web sites will have a greater impact on your Web site's search engine rankings than one or two links from high-ranking sites.

There are a number of ways you can obtain quality links for your Web site. Here are a few techniques you can use to help your Web site gain visibility through Web site links.

Participate in Blogrings

In Chapter 4, you learned how you could build a network of fellow creative businesspeople and gain access to their online customers by joining blogrings. This network can also help you by giving you the ability to impress other creative people enough that they are willing to link to your business Web site from theirs.

Asking a fellow artist for a link directly is considered in poor taste in the Internet community. To refer back to the high school analogy, this is tantamount to begging for friends. It rarely works and may serve only to lower the level of respect that other online artists have for you.

Instead, concentrate on creating artworks, images, and content so compelling that fellow artists willingly link to your Web site because they want to be associated with someone as talented and professional as you. This will help you obtain links not only from fellow artists in your blogring, but also from people you have never met who are so impressed with your artwork that they want to make sure their friends, customers, and Web site visitors know about you.

You can also try contacting other creative businesspeople online, telling them you enjoy their work and asking if they would mind if you linked to their site. Assuming that they agree, there is a good chance they will reciprocate by providing a link to your Web site as well. Using the high school scenario, this amounts to gaining friends by flattery, but it works far better than contacting other artists and making unsolicited requests for links.

Participate in Online Discussion Forums

This technique is similar to using blogs and blogrings to obtain inbound links, but instead of using your blog to promote your Web site, you use online discussion forums.

Online discussion forums are Web sites, or sections of larger Web sites, on which people gather to discuss a topic or several related topics. These discussions occur in the form of short posts that are gathered in sequential order — a sequence of posts on a particular subtopic is called a thread. Essentially, one discussion board member starts a subtopic thread under a broader topic category with a single post, and then other members respond with their opinions and thoughts. As the discussion progresses, the conversation may become a collection of thoughts about the subtopic, or it may meander through a series of even more narrowly defined subtopics, until a consensus is reached or everyone gets bored with the discussion.

Although most discussion boards will not allow individual members to promote a business Web site within the text of a post, they will allow you to promote your Web site in the signature line of your posts or in your personal member profile. A signature line is a space below each post you create where you can include quotes, information, and hyperlinks. You do not have to type the signature line each time you post — it will be added automatically.

The signature line should not make it obvious that you are trying to get Web site visitors (and links). Just write your signature line as though you were providing an informational link — something that might be beneficial to anyone interested.

Here is how a discussion forum post may look with a signature line promoting Joe Smith's art Web site:

Water-soluble oil paints seem to work well for beginners, but in my experience, they just do not have the right consistency for blending properly. They always seem to end up creating choppy color blends — kind of like cheap acrylics. I realize others here have had better luck with these paints, but again, that has just been my own personal experience. Maybe I am doing something wrong — feel free to make suggestions.

If you enjoy abstract art and earth tone palettes, visit www. joesmithartstudio.com. I would appreciate your feedback and suggestions about the Web site.

After fellow discussion board members see this signature line enough times, they will be compelled to click on the link, where they can learn more about your creative business and admire the professionalism and creativity of your work. Because they have gotten to know you through the online discussion board, they will not think twice about linking to your Web site from their own personal or business Web site.

Of course, you can also use this method to ask fellow artists if you can link to their sites in the hope that they will reciprocate. This can be a good way to build a number of relevant links that will help you improve your Web site's search engine rankings while making new friends along the way.

The topic of promoting your business through participation in discussion board postings will be covered more thoroughly in Chapter 9.

Buy Links

Another uncomfortable truth that carries over from high school to the Internet is contained in the adage, "If you can't make friends, you can always buy them." Fortunately, this adage carries less of a stigma on the Internet than it does in secondary education. There are a number of Web sites where you can purchase inbound links from high-ranking, quality Web sites. Many of these are link brokerages, which solicit high-ranking Web sites to provide links and sell the rights to these links to other Web site owners. These offerings are sometimes displayed and sold in an online auction format, or the Web site may simply have set pricing for each link. The rights to the inbound links may last one month, although you can purchase the rights to the links for as many months as your budget will allow.

The prices for these links can be rather steep, depending on the quality and popularity of the linking Web site, the fees charged by the link broker, and whether your link will appear on the Web site's home page or a secondary page. You can buy a link on a secondary page of a moderately successful Web site for less than $20 per month, or you can pay more than $800 per month to have a link to your Web site featured on a high-ranking, well-respected Web site with high daily traffic.

If you are willing to pay for inbound links to help increase your Web site's search engine rankings, here are some brokerage Web sites that specialize in providing high-quality links:

- You can find thousands of Web sites willing to link to yours at **www.linkadage.com**. This site features an auction format and does not charge fees to the buyer above the winning bid amount. However, this Web site does charge listing fees up to $24.99 and final value fees up to 10 percent of the winning bid, which tends to drive up minimum-bid prices for higher-quality links.

- Another option that gives you plenty of Web sites to choose from is **www.textlinkbrokers.com**. This Web site gives you the Alexa search engine ranking for each link provider and gives you different pricing options for each available page on a link provider's Web site. Although it provides a more comprehensive approach to providing relevant links to buyers, this Web site does not disclose the fees paid by link providers.

- ☙ You can search for Web sites with content relevant to yours at **www.livecustomer.com**. This Web site uses an inventory format rather than an online auction format. This Web site does not disclose fees paid by link providers.

Link Building Techniques to Avoid

Unlike unethical keyword usage, there are not currently any link building techniques that will get your Web site banned from search engine listings. There are, however, several techniques that are a waste of time, money, or both. Here are a few link building techniques that will serve only to frustrate you.

Using Link Farms

Link farms are Web sites that promise to get you hundreds of quality links for an outrageously low fee. What happens is that your Web site is entered into a pool of other Web sites, with every one providing a link to every other Web site in that pool. The Web site owners (including you) will not know which other Web sites a site is linking to, because the linking is done via automated software rather than by placing manual links on the Web pages.

You may be able to obtain 200 inbound links for your art Web site from a link farm, but it will not help your Web site rankings if the links are from Web sites owned by sheep herders in rural

Ireland or factories in Detroit. Search engine spiders consider these links to be irrelevant and disregard them when calculating the ranking of your Web pages.

In the future, Google and other search engines may choose to penalize Web sites that use link farms to generate inbound links, rather than just ignoring the irrelevant links. No one is certain if the search engines will begin to use these links to lower individual Web site rankings or ban Web sites from search engine listings altogether, but it is best to avoid link farms in case this ever occurs. At the least, avoiding these sites will save you a substantial amount of time and money.

Linking to Your Own Web Site

Almost every Web site owner that has dabbled in search engine optimization techniques has thought at least once about creating blogs or separate Web sites for the sole purpose of providing inbound links to a main Web site.

Although this technique will not hurt your search engine rankings for your main Web site, it will not improve your rankings, either. Unless the secondary sites or blogs you are linking from have high traffic volume and links from other high-ranking sites, this exercise will serve only to waste time you could be using to create your artworks or employ more useful techniques to help you grow your business.

As noted earlier in this chapter, there is nothing wrong with providing links to your Web site from your signature line on discussion board posts or from a related blog that you post to frequently. The links themselves may have little value in determining your search engine rankings, but they are valuable tools for getting the people who are reading your posts to click on the links and visit your Web site.

Now let us move on to outsourcing the creation of content for your Web site, blogs, and articles, if you are not comfortable with creating the content yourself.

Outsourcing: What To Do If You Are Not A Writer

In Chapter 4, you learned how to create Web site content that will help your business's site gain a better position in search engine rankings, bring traffic from other Web sites, and attract attention from discussion boards and other online forums. This may seem like a daunting task, particularly if your creative skills do not extend to writing. What should you do if you are not a writer and you want to be able to create and upload your artworks, without having to agonize over every word on your Web site, blog posts, and articles?

Fortunately, it is easy to get other people to do this work for you, if you are willing to make a modest investment. You do not have to hire a nationally known copywriting firm to create your content and pay them thousands of dollars to get your Web site noticed. There are thousands of talented freelance writers available on the Internet who can create keyword-optimized, compelling content for you at reasonable rates.

Elance

A good Web site for finding freelance writers to create your Web site and blog content is **www.elance.com**. There are thousands of freelance writers from dozens of countries that specialize in creating Web site, blog, and article copy. Many of these writers also understand the content strategies required to obtain excellent search engine rankings, so investing in a freelance writer will not only help you get Web site content that your visitors will enjoy, it will also help you rank high in search engine listings without requiring you to spend long evenings trying to learn the nuances of Web site optimization.

There are a few different ways you can use Elance to find the right freelance writer for you. First, you can open a free buyer account and post a project under Elance's Writing and Translation category. Depending on how quickly you need your Web site or blog content, you can post your project for three, seven, or ten days. The longer your project appears in Elance's listings, the greater number of freelance writers will see your project.

Projects posted on Elance work in a reverse auction fashion — instead of buyers competing to purchase an item, freelance writers compete to win the right to complete your project.

Your Project Description

Once you have decided you want a freelance writer to complete your Web site or blog content, set aside a half hour to draft your project description. There is no required format for a description, but a comprehensive and detailed project description will help you get more qualified bidders and increases your chances of being happy with the end result. The time you spend creating a detailed project description will also pay off in terms of spending less time asking your freelance writer to make revisions or answering frequent questions from your winning bidder.

To illustrate, suppose you are freelance writer seeking projects to bid on. You see two projects that require keyword-optimized content for an art Web site. The project description for the first one reads:

> I am launching a Web site to sell my art. I need keyword-optimized content completed within two weeks.

You move on to the second project and read the following description:

> Established artist seeks a writer to provide keyword-optimized content for a Web site that will launch in about three weeks. Here are the content pages I will require:

⊙ **A home page**, which will introduce the Web site visitors to my artwork. The content on this page should invite visitors to explore the site, without telling them every detail about my art or my career as an artist. This page should focus on creating a professional image so that visitors will feel comfortable doing business with me. I will send you an image of the artwork that will be displayed on the home page — this should help you establish the tone.

- **An About Me page**, which will tell visitors about my background and artistic vision and will detail my professional achievements as an artist. I will provide some notes to help you get started on this page.

- **A Frequently Asked Questions page**. I have a list of questions and answers and will need you to expand on my answers and optimize this page using keywords I will supply.

- **A Thank You page**, which will display after a visitor places an order for an artwork. This page should emphasize the quality of the work they have just purchased and make the buyer feel special for having procured such a unique piece of artwork. The purposes of this page are to minimize the number of returned artworks and to encourage repeat business.

This project will need to be completed in two weeks or less. Thank you for bidding on this project.

The first project description does not tell your potential bidders much about the project. As a result, you will either spend your time answering questions from potential bidders or wondering why few freelancers are bidding on your project.

The second description makes your expectations clear to potential bidders. This helps you obtain better results because bidders can more easily determine whether your project matches their skill sets and whether the project is too large for them to take on.

Your Project Budget

When you post a project on Elance, you will be asked to supply a budget for your project. These budgets do not commit you to spending a specific dollar amount; rather, they provide a range for your bidders to use as a guideline — less than $250, $250 to $500, $500 to $750 or higher. You can also elect not to disclose a budget, but you can expect to see some unreasonable bid amounts if you choose this option.

The minimum bid amount on Elance is $50, so if you are seeking content for less than that amount, you need to find another means of finding a freelance writer.

Freelancers charge significantly different amounts for their services, depending on their level of expertise, length of experience, and how highly they value their own work. You can expect to pay between $5 and $15 per page for Web site and blog content, including keyword optimization. You will find some freelancers who will work for less than $5 per page, but if you are considering one of these bidders, you should ask to see several samples of his or her previous writing before you commit to working with this person.

Selecting a Winning Bidder

When your project closes, you will have an opportunity to review the bids submitted by potential writers. There are several things you should consider when evaluating bidders for your project:

Bid Descriptions

Bidders can provide details about their bids in one of two ways — in the bid description field that shows beneath your project description and in private message boards that can be seen only by you and the individual bidder.

Bid descriptions should highlight the bidders' experience, provide evidence that the bidder understands the scope and subject matter of your project, and give details of what the bidder will provide.

The bid descriptions should also give you a basic understanding of each bidder's writing ability. If a bidder submits a description that contains grammatical or spelling errors, it shows that the bidder may not possess the attention to detail or the understanding of the English language necessary to complete your project.

Writing Samples

You should always require writing samples from each bidder. If a bidder does not provide writing samples, it may be an indication that the bidder does not have experience writing the type of content you require or that the bidder is aware his or her writing skills are deficient. Use extreme caution when considering a bidder who fails to include writing samples with his or her bid.

You can use writing samples that are included with bids to evaluate the ability of each writer. These samples will give you an understanding of each bidder's writing ability and a sense of each writer's style. If a bidder submits multiple samples that reflect different writing styles, this may be an indication that the writer is sufficiently versatile to handle many types of projects.

If a bidder submits samples that reflect correct spelling and grammar but are not relevant to your project, you can ask the bidder to submit an additional sample on a topic you select. Bidders who are serious about completing your project will be happy to submit an additional sample to assure you that they are the perfect writer for you.

Bid Amounts

The project fees included by writers in bid descriptions should be within your project budget. Some bidders choose to ignore project budgets and bid their usual fees. Although the work of some of the bidders may be worth an amount above your project budget, posting a bid amount outside your project budget shows a potential lack of attention to detail. If you are interested in the work of a bidder that posts a bid amount over your budget, ask the bidder why he or she feels the additional fees are justified.

When reviewing bids that are within your project budget, you should consider each bid amount within the context of the individual writer's ability. If your stated project budget is between $250 and $500, a bidder who posts a $500 bid should be able to demonstrate that his or her work is substantially better than a bidder who posts a bid of $250. If he or she can do this, it may be worth the extra money to hire a writer who can produce superior work with few mistakes.

Although Elance does not charge fees to buyers for posting or accepting projects, this Web site charges fees to providers. Writers and other professionals on Elance are charged monthly membership fees, which can range from $11 to nearly $100 per month. In addition, Elance charges providers a percentage of the money they make from completing projects — these percentage-based fees range from 6.25 to 8.25 percent of the income derived from Elance projects. Thus, do not be surprised if bidders expect to be paid well for their services, because a substantial portion of their fees go toward paying for the privilege of doing business on Elance.

Bidder Reviews and Feedback

Elance provides a means for buyers and providers to give feedback for each other based on the quality of work and performance demonstrated in past projects.

Elance also allows buyers to rate providers on a number of criteria, using a numerical scale from one (poor performance) to five (excellent performance). These scores are then averaged to produce a provider's score for a particular project.

You can use these scores, along with the feedback provided by past buyers, to see how a writer has performed on projects. Several low scores mean several buyers have had problems with a particular writer, so it may be best not to choose this bidder for your project. Consistently high scores, on the other hand, mean the bidder has met or exceeded his or her commitments for many buyers and will likely meet his or her commitments to you as well.

Working with Your Wining Bidder

Once you have selected a freelance writer who can work within your budget and with whom you feel comfortable, you should establish a good working relationship with your writer. It is a good idea to contact your writer through Elance as soon as possible after you award the project to him or her. You can use this first contact to accomplish three things:

- ⊛ It allows you to make sure your writer is still interested in the project and still has time to complete the work. Business on Elance moves quickly — freelancers can go from having an open schedule to being completely booked with projects in a day or two. Your writer may have accepted other projects between placing a bid on yours and receiving your project award notification. Contacting the winning bidder immediately after awarding the project will help minimize the delay if you have to choose another bidder.

- ⊛ It lets you forward project details that you chose not to include in your project description. This may include proprietary information about your artworks or your business model, reference Web sites for your writer to review for comparison, personal biographical information, or your commission fee structure.

- ⊛ It gives you the opportunity to let your writer know you are open to questions while he or she is completing the project. Although you do not want to be inundated with questions about every facet of the project, it takes far less time to answer a few questions before the project starts than to wait for revisions when your writer delivers content that is different than you envisioned.

Another excellent way to make sure your project progresses smoothly is to ask your writer to set up milestones for completion of the work. For example, if you need your writer to provide content for four pages on your Web site, your writer could set up four milestones, with 25 percent of the payment due on the completion of each milestone. This allows you to review the work as it progresses, instead of receiving all the content at once and discovering it is incorrect. It also allows you to terminate the agreement if your writer is unable or unwilling to make revisions. If you plan to reserve the right to terminate the project early, make sure you communicate this to the winning bidder before the project begins.

Guru

You can also find hundreds of writing professionals at **www. guru.com.** This Web site works in much the same manner as Elance — the main difference is the fees it charges to providers. The monthly membership fees tend to be a little higher than those charged by Elance, but the percentage fees charged for income derived from Guru is a little lower.

The result of this difference is that Guru attracts a greater percentage of writer teams, which means several people share the costs of monthly membership fees. It also means, if you award a project to one of these provider teams, your project may be assigned to one of many members of that team — not necessarily the one who wrote the writing samples for you.

The benefit of working with a writing team through Guru is that several writers may have input that will make the content you receive better than if you relied on a sole provider to understand your ideas and translate them into Web site content. The drawback is you may not get to choose the writer who executes the production of the content.

Other Freelancing Web Sites

There are dozens of other Web sites you can use to find a freelance writer to provide content for your Web site, articles, or blog posts. You can check **www.gofreelance.com, www.freelancewriting. com**, and **www.sologig.com** for experienced writers. Since most freelance writing Web sites allow buyers to post projects for free, you can post your project on multiple Web sites and compare bids from each.

Keep in mind, though, that some of these sites keep track of your ratio of projects awarded to projects posted and provide these ratios to potential bidders. This means that, if you post many projects on one of these Web sites but award few, providers will notice this and will be less likely to submit bids on future projects. On Elance and other freelance writing Web sites, providers are allotted a limited number of bids each month, so an individual provider may not want to use a bid to post on a project if you have a history of posting projects but not awarding them to bidders.

Getting Your Web Site Into Search Engines & Directories

Submitting Your Web Site to Search Engines

Even if you have taken all the necessary steps to include keywords in your content, title and meta tags, image tags, and page descriptions, your Web site will not be likely to receive much traffic if you do not submit your Web site to search engines.

Fortunately, there are only a few search engines to which you absolutely need to submit your Web site. With the exception of some small regional search engines, most of the lesser-known engines draw results from one of the three main search engines: Google, MSN Search, and Yahoo!. Some are also meta search engines, which are search sites that do not contain search results but rather perform live searches across the Web to provide results from multiple search engines.

Some rather enterprising people have realized that quite a few people do not understand that most search engines obtain their results from the same few sites. Thus, you will find companies advertising on the Internet that promise to submit your Web site to hundreds of search engines for a fixed or recurring fee. They will promise to save you many hours in submission and resubmission time; however, you can easily submit your Web site to search engines yourself in just a few minutes and avoid paying the fees these companies charge.

Unless you are concerned with establishing a regional presence on a local search engine, you can gain all the search exposure you need by submitting your Web site to Google, MSN Search, and Yahoo! and letting the other search engines and meta search engines pick up your Web site from results compiled by those three sites.

Here are instructions for submitting your Web site to the three main search engines:

Google

Submitting your Web site to Google's search engine is a simple process. Type the following URL into your browser:

www.google.com/addurl

Once you have accessed this submission page, you will need to fill in three text boxes to submit your site. The first text box is for the address of your Web site. Be sure to include http:// in front of your Web site address. For example, if your site's address is www.joesmithartstudio.com, you should enter the address like this:

http://www.joesmithartstudio.com

The second box is for comments or keywords that describe your Web site. These are only informational comments for Google staff and will not help your page rankings in any way. You can choose to leave this box blank; however, filling in this box should only take a couple of minutes, so it is a good idea to complete this step in case Google encounters any problems indexing your Web site.

The third box requires you to enter a series of letters and numbers shown in a graphic above the box. Google requires this so that robots, which cannot read the characters shown in the graphic, cannot automatically submit sites to the search engine.

MSN Search

Submitting your Web site to MSN Live Search is also an easy process. Simply type the following URL into your Web browser:

http://search.msn.com.sg/docs/submit.aspx

On this page, you need to fill in the first field with the letters and numbers shown in the graphic above the box and the second field with your Web site address. Do not forget to type http:// before the Web site address, or the submission page will not recognize your entry as a valid Web site address.

Yahoo! Search

Submitting your Web site to Yahoo! Search is a simple task, but unlike Google and MSN, Yahoo! requires you to have a valid Yahoo! e-mail address before you can complete your submission.

To sign up for a Yahoo! account, go to the Yahoo! home page at **www.yahoo.com** and click on the "Mail" button on the right side of the page. The next page will prompt you to enter your login ID and password or sign up for a new account. Click on the Sign Up link, and you will be taken to a new page on which you will fill in your contact information and choose a new ID and password.

Once you have created your Yahoo! e-mail address, type the following URL into your Web browser:

https://siteexplorer.search.yahoo.com/submit

On this page, you need to enter your Web site address, beginning with http://, and your site submission will be complete.

When submitting your Web site to the three major search engines, it is important to remember that frequent resubmission of your site can be viewed as spamming by the search engines. Even if your Web site content changes frequently, you will want to resubmit your site to the search engines no more than once per month. This will keep the search engines from penalizing your

Web site by downgrading the site's search engine ranking or by removing your site from the search listings altogether.

Yahoo! Search Directory

You can also submit your Web site to the Yahoo! Search Directory, which allows users to search for Web sites based on a number of categories. A search directory differs from a search engine in that Web sites submitted for inclusion are reviewed by human editors, rather than crawled by search engine spiders.

The editors who review your Web site will evaluate your site's content for appropriateness and will choose the category and subcategory under which your Web site will be placed.

Because Web sites submitted to the Yahoo! Search Directory are reviewed and indexed by humans, it is easier for people to find your Web site through a search directory than through a search engine. A directory user will find far fewer irrelevant results and will find better content because of the intensive site review Yahoo! performs on each Web site submitted for inclusion.

The benefit of including your Web site in the Yahoo! Search Directory is that your Web site will not only get more traffic, but also better-quality traffic. People who use directory searches have a clearer idea of what they are looking for than search engine users, and the directory helps them find exactly what they are looking for.

The drawback of submitting your Web site to the Yahoo! Search directory is that, while you can submit your Web site to search engines for free or at a low cost, Yahoo! charges fees for directory submissions.

Submitting a Web site that does not contain adult content currently costs $299, and directory submission of a Web site that does contain adult content costs $600. These fees are nonrefundable, regardless of whether your Web site is accepted for inclusion to the Yahoo! Search Directory.

If your Web site is accepted, Yahoo! will charge you a yearly fee, equal to the amount you paid for directory submission, for continuing to list your Web site in the Yahoo! Search Directory.

To submit your Web site to the Yahoo! search directory, type the following URL into your Web browser:

http://search.yahoo.com/info/submit.html

Click on the Yahoo! Directory Submit link near the bottom of the page. The next page will tell you a little about how the review process works. Click the Get Started link on this page.

You will then need to enter your Yahoo! e-mail address and password. If you do not have a Yahoo! ID, you will need to create one, which is detailed previously.

After you have entered your Yahoo! ID and password, you will be redirected to a page on which you will verify whether your site contains adult content and accept the Terms of Service. You will then enter your Web site information, including category suggestions and a description of your Web site's content.

After you have paid for the directory submission, Yahoo! editors will review and index your site within about seven days so you will start generating traffic quickly.

Open Directory Project

Another option for directory submission is the Open Directory Project, where you can submit your Web site and have it reviewed by human editors for inclusion. Submission to the Open Directory Project is free, and the content requirements are significantly less stringent than those of the Yahoo! Search Directory.

The more lenient submission requirements and the free nature of this directory mean there are far more Web sites listed in the Open Directory Project than in Yahoo! Search Directory, so it will be more difficult for a directory user to find your Web site. You will still receive more targeted traffic through this directory than through a search engine, but the Open Project Directory will not be as useful for your business as the Yahoo! Search Directory. If cost containment is an important factor to your Internet marketing efforts, though, this can be a good way to gain exposure for your Web site.

To submit your site to the Open Directory Project, visit **www. dmoz.org**. Select a category and a subcategory and enter your Web site information. Once you submit your site, Open Directory editors will review and index your site within a few weeks.

Software & Web Services for Running Your Business: The Tools of Success

Like any professional, an artist building an online business needs tools to be successful and profitable. Imagine a carpenter showing up to build an addition to your house but not having a saw, a hammer, or a measuring tape. The chances of that person doing the job correctly, or even getting it done, are slim. Similarly, without certain tools, it will be difficult for you to build a viable online business.

This chapter will tell you about several tools you can use to build your business more quickly and easily while saving money and frustration along the way. Some of these tools can be acquired along the way, as your business begins to generate a profit; others are essential to getting started and will be of little use if you try to use them after your business is already up and running.

You will also learn the approximate cost of each of these tools so you can budget for them while you are building your online presence.

Web Site Creation Tools

Unless you use a template-based site builder offered by your Web site host or you have extensive knowledge of Web site coding languages, such as HTML and JavaScript, you will need a Web site creation tool to properly design your site and make sure all the elements of your site are functional. There are several Web site creation tools available that can make designing your Web site a simple and relatively quick process.

Microsoft Expression Studio

Microsoft Expression Studio consists of a suite of tools that can help you easily create Web pages, design content for your Web site, and manage your data files for easy retrieval. Here are the four programs included with Microsoft Expression Studio:

Microsoft Expression Web

This application allows you to create Web pages via a WYSIWYG (What You See Is What You Get) interface. This means that instead of requiring you to manually code your Web pages in HTML or other Internet language, Expression Web allows you to point and click to decide where you want text, images, links, and other Web site elements. While you are building your pages, Expression Web will create HTML code designed to make sure your Web site will display correctly on all browsers.

If you do have HTML programming experience, you can also toggle between Expression Web's WYSIWYG interface and the site's HTML code to fine-tune your Web site's design and functionality.

Microsoft Expression Blend

Microsoft Expression Blend allows you to seamlessly place sophisticated media files within your Web pages. You can use Expression Blend to integrate animations, text with high-quality and nonstandard fonts, vector graphics, video, and three-dimensional effects into your site design. Expression Blend converts vector and bitmap graphics to XAML format, making integration of complex image file types a simple process.

Microsoft Expression Design

The Microsoft Expression Design tool lets you create the media and image files you will integrate into your Web site via the Microsoft Blend application. You can create seamless video, high-quality vector graphics, animation files, and more for your Web site. These files capture the interest of your Web site visitors and help keep them on your site longer so they will be more inclined to purchase your creative works.

Microsoft Expression Media

If you are building a complex Web site with multiple pages and galleries, you likely have hundreds or even thousands of files to keep track of. Microsoft Expression Media is a tool for categorizing, managing, and storing these files so you can easily find and retrieve the exact files you want while you are building or updating your Web site.

This is particularly important for managing online gallery pages, which will need to be updated frequently to showcase new creative works and remove the works you have sold.

Although Microsoft Expression Studio offers several powerful tools for building a dynamic and user-friendly Web site, it can be a little expensive for an artist just starting out on the Internet. You can purchase this suite of Web site tools on **www.microsoft.com/ expression** for $599, or you can also find Microsoft Expression Studio on **www.amazon.com** for about $560.

If you think you may want to create a unique, complex site rich with graphic and video features but you do not want to pay a developer to create your Web site for you, Microsoft Expression Web may be worth the substantial investment.

Before getting out your credit card to order Microsoft Expression Web, though, you may want to download a free trial version of the software suite from **www.microsoft.com/expression**. You can try the software applications for 60 days, which will give you time to learn how to use the various features and start building your Web site. Keep in mind, though, that if you do not purchase Microsoft Expression Studio at the end of your trial period, you will not be able to retrieve the Web pages you have created while using the trial software.

Adobe Dreamweaver CS3

Adobe Dreamweaver CS3 gives you much of the same functionality as Microsoft Expression Studio, but it combines all its features into one software application. You can toggle between the WYSIWYG interface and the HTML or XHTML code for your Web site so you can create your site exactly the way you want.

You can use CSS style sheets for your site, which are sections of code that allow you to easily make each page of your Web site follow the same design style without having to manually match up the colors and element placements on each page. Dreamweaver CS3 also features a browser validation tool that checks to make sure your Web site layout is compatible with all browser types.

If you intend to integrate video into your Web site, Dreamweaver CS3 gives you the ability to incorporate Adobe Flash video files into your Web pages with just a few mouse clicks. This is a significant advantage over other types of Web site creation tools, which can make video integration a tedious and frustrating process.

Dreamweaver CS3 is also a good choice if you use a Macintosh as your main computer. This Web site creation tool is designed to be compatible with both Windows-based systems and Macintosh systems.

If you purchase Adobe Dreamweaver CS3 directly from the manufacturer's Web site at **www.adobe.com/products/**

dreamweaver, you can expect to pay about $600 for this software; however, you can find Dreamweaver CS3 on **www.amazon.com** for as little as $399.

Like Microsoft Expressions Studio, Adobe Dreamweaver CS3 is available as a trial download but for 45 days. Go to **www. adobe.com/products/dreamweaver**.

PageBreeze

If Adobe Dreamweaver CS3 and Microsoft Expressions Studio are a little expensive for your marketing budget, then consider using PageBreeze to build your Web site. PageBreeze is a free Web site creation tool available for download at **www.pagebreeze.com.** There are no time restrictions or hidden fees associated with your PageBreeze download — you can use the free software as long as you like and build as many Web sites and Web pages as you want.

The software is not as sophisticated as Dreamweaver CS3 or Expression Web, but it gives you the ability to build your Web site via both a WYSIWYG interface and an HTML coding page. It also allows you to use CSS to create style sheets to make sure the pages of your Web site complement each other.

You can easily import graphics from Adobe Photoshop®, Paint Shop Pro, or another graphics program, as long as you save the graphics in a JPEG or GIF format. Adding these graphics to your Web site is as simple as clicking where you want the graphic to appear in your Web page and clicking "Insert Graphic" on the PageBreeze toolbar.

Adding text to your Web pages is simple as well. Just click the area on your Web page where you want the text to appear and start typing. If you want multiple columns of text on a Web Page or you want to create a sidebar where you can provide links or featured information, just click "Tables" on the toolbar and select the number of columns you want. You can make the table borders invisible so they do not appear on your finished Web page.

Although PageBreeze lacks some of the versatility of Dreamweaver CS3 or Expression Web, you can easily alter the HTML code to change Web page elements that you cannot create in WYSIWYG mode.

For example, PageBreeze offers a limited number of text fonts — while you are in WYSIWIG mode, you are limited to Arial, Times New Roman, Courier, Tahoma, Verdana, and Wingdings. However, if you switch to HTML mode, you can change the font to any font that is browser supported (this includes almost all fonts used in popular word processing programs). You can use Microsoft Word or another word processing program to find a font appropriate for your Web site.

Once you have found a font you like, look through the HTML code for references to the font you used in WYSIWYG mode and replace them with the name of your new font.

To illustrate, here is an example of a piece of HTML code generated in PageBreeze:

```
<p align="center"> </p>
```

```
<p align="center"><font face="Arial" size="4"><strong>Thank You!</strong></font></p>
```

```
<p align="center"><font face="Arial" size="4">I appreciate your artwork commission request. Please check your inbox for a confirmation e-mail -- I will not receive your request until you click the link in the confirmation e-mail.</font></p>
```

```
<p align="center"><font face="Arial" size="4">Once I receive your request, I will contact you to discuss your vision for the artwork in greater detail. </font></p>
```

```
<p align="center"><font face="Arial" size="4">I look forward to creating a custom artwork that will complement your home and bring you many years of enjoyment.</font></p>
```

Although this may look intimidating if you have never worked with HTML, you do not need to be concerned with the majority of this code. Just look for the references to Arial font.

Let us suppose you have decided Papyrus font would be appropriate for the look and feel of your Web site. All you would need to do is replace all the references to Arial with Papyrus.

```
<p align="center"> </p>
```

```
<p align="center"><font face="Papyrus" size="4"><strong>Thank You!</strong></font></p>
```

```
<p align="center"><font face="Papyrus" size="4">I appreciate
```
your artwork commission request. Please check your inbox for a confirmation e-mail -- I will not receive your request until you click the link in the confirmation e-mail.`</font></p>

```
<p align="center"><font face="Papyrus" size="4">Once I
```
receive your request, I will contact you to discuss your vision for the artwork in greater detail. `</font></p>

```
<p align="center"><font face="Papyrus" size="4">I look
```
forward to creating a custom artwork that will complement your home and bring you many years of enjoyment.`</font></p>

Click the save button, and then the text in your Web page associated with this section of HTML code will display in Papyrus font.

You can make similar adjustments to font sizes, table widths, and other elements that may be difficult to perfect in WYSIWYG mode. You will also need to use the HTML mode to insert video or JavaScript elements into your Web pages. Do not worry; you can use other software or Web applications to generate the code you will need to integrate these elements into your Web pages so you will not have to worry about coding it yourself.

Again, working with PageBreeze can be a little more cumbersome than working with Dreamweaver CS3 or Expressions Studio, but if you are building a fairly simple Web site and are not afraid to fine-tune the HTML code for your pages, PageBreeze can be an economical way to design your Web site and achieve professional results.

CGI Form and Autoresponder Tools

Your Web site is one of the most important elements of your art business's marketing strategy. However, to generate repeat visitors, you will need to use a means of reminding your visitors of your presence and enticing them to return to your Web site through discounts, special offers, and announcements of your new creative works. The easiest way to do this is to provide a way for your Web site visitors to enter their e-mail addresses on your site and to compile these e-mail addresses into marketing lists so you can create e-mail announcements.

A CGI form is a text field you can place on your Web site so that your visitors can enter their contact details or other information. You can use CGI forms to ask visitors for their names, e-mail addresses, telephone numbers, favorite types of artworks, or any other type of information you can use in your marketing efforts.

Once a Web site visitor has entered his or her contact information into a CGI form on your Web site, it will be transmitted to a CGI bin, which formats the information submitted by the visitor and sends it to your e-mail address. You can then transfer the information to a database, which you can use to easily send e-mail messages to an entire group of people with just the click of a mouse.

Because federal laws prohibit the use of spam, or transmission of unsolicited e-mail messages, you should always couple CGI forms with a pre-written e-mail requiring visitors to confirm they have voluntarily submitted their contact information and that they consent to receiving e-mail messages from you. This will help save you from receiving numerous complaints from people who completed a CGI form on your Web site but have since forgotten that they did so.

Autoresponders are e-mail programs that allow you to compose e-mails and have them sent as soon as a visitor completes a CGI form on your Web site and at specified time intervals thereafter. This can save you hours of time, because you can set up your e-mail messages once and never have to worry about checking for new subscribers and manually sending them a series of e-mails.

There are several applications that can help you place CGI forms on your Web site and automatically send e-mail messages to them to promote your artworks, announce discounts and specials, and provide your subscribers with useful information to establish your position as a professional artist.

FormBreeze

FormBreeze is a CGI form generator and autoresponder system that is designed for use with the PageBreeze Web site creation tool. FormBreeze offers the PageBreeze tool for free, knowing that a certain percentage of PageBreeze users will subscribe to the FormBreeze service.

FormBreeze allows you to easily create visitor input forms for use on you Web site and provides unlimited autoresponders to send e-mail messages to subscribers that complete your Web forms.

You can customize your autoresponder messages to be sent at specified intervals. For example, you may create a confirmation e-mail that will be sent as soon as a visitor completes a CGI Web form, a welcome message that will be sent as soon as the visitor confirms his or her subscription, and sales e-mails every other day for the next two weeks to help familiarize your subscriber with your creative works. You can also create broadcast e-mails that will be sent to all your current subscribers at once, so you can alert them of new artworks or discounts that will be available for only a limited time.

FormBreeze allows you to collect statistics about your subscribers, such as the percentage of subscribers that open an autoresponder e-mail, the number of subscribers that click on a link contained in an e-mail, and the number of people that unsubscribe from your mailing lists. This can help you understand how well your e-mail marketing efforts are working so you can make adjustments on future e-mail campaigns.

FormBreeze offers two subscription packages: The first allows you to create up to three CGI forms with unlimited autoresponder messages for $6.99 per month; the second allows you to create up to ten CGI forms with unlimited autoresponder messages for $19.99 per month. Unless you have more than one Web site for your creative works, it is unlikely that you will need more than three CGI forms; however, if you plan on expanding your e-mail marketing efforts in the future, the second package may be a useful solution.

AWeber Communications

AWeber is another tool you can use to create CGI forms, place the forms on your Web site, and create autoresponder messages to be sent to people who complete and submit the forms.

With AWeber, you can create several types of CGI forms, depending on how aggressively you want to pursue e-mail marketing. Like FormBreeze, you can create a simple CGI form that can be placed anywhere on your Web pages, giving Web site visitors the option to subscribe to your newsletters or obtain free informational products. AWeber also gives you the ability to create CGI forms that pop up when a visitor opens a Web page on your site, making the form the focal point of the page until the visitor completes and submits the form or closes the pop-up box. You can also create exit pop-up forms, which prompt a visitor to enter contact information when he or she navigates away from your Web site.

Pop-up and exit pop-up CGI forms can be good tools if your marketing focus includes aggressive e-mail marketing, but they have some drawbacks. First, they are viewed by some Web site visitors as intrusive and may cause you to lose repeat visitors because of the aggressiveness associated with pop-ups. Second, they can easily be disabled by a pop-up blocker, which is a software application that detects pop-ups and disables them before they can be seen by a Web site visitor. Pop-up blockers will dilute the effectiveness of these CGI forms, because many of your Web site visitors will not see them and will not have an opportunity to subscribe to your marketing list.

AWeber also gives you the ability to create and manage autoresponder messages for each CGI form you create. You can write a series of e-mail messages and configure an autoresponder to send the messages at specified intervals. You can also write broadcast messages that will be sent to all your current subscribers at a specified time.

You will also have access to statistical information about the use of messages you create — you can find out how many people opened an e-mail message, clicked on a link within the message, or deleted the message without opening it.

AWeber is a good choice if you plan on creating multiple e-mail campaigns and creating multiple CGI forms. It gives you an easy interface to view and manage all your campaigns at once, which can save you quite a bit of time.

There is only one package available through AWeber — you get unlimited CGI forms and unlimited autoresponder messages for $19.99 per month. You can subscribe to this service at **www. aweber.com**.

GetResponse

GetResponse offers all the same features and tools as AWeber — you can easily create CGI forms, create and configure autoresponder messages, and manage your e-mail marketing campaigns via an intuitive interface. The main difference is pricing for a large volume of subscribers — both providers charge additional monthly fees if you have more than 10,000 subscribers to your e-mail marketing lists. Although the package offered by

GetResponse is slightly more expensive than AWeber's package at $22.95 per month, AWeber charges an additional $9.95 per month if you have more than 10,000 subscribers, while GetResponse charges an additional $4.95 per month.

Any Internet marketer would agree that a list of 10,000 subscribers is impressive and takes a long time to build. However, if you plan to build a large marketing list, GetResponse may be a good solution for you.

You will learn more about creating e-mail marketing campaigns and newsletters in Chapter 10.

Visitor Tracking Software

If you want your Web site to be a success and generate sufficient sales to derive a full-time income from your creative works online, you will need to have a means to determine how well your Web site is performing. There are a number of tools you can use to analyze the traffic on your Web site so you can predict your site's success and make modifications to your site to increase its performance. Here are some of the tools that are available for tracking the traffic on your site.

StatCounter

StatCounter is a free tool you can use to analyze the traffic on your Web site and learn how you can improve your Web site's content to generate additional traffic. You can register for a free account at **www.statcounter.com**. The registration process takes just a few minutes — you will enter your contact information and a few details about your Web site, and you will have access to several features that can help you determine the success of your site.

Once you have registered your account, StatCounter will generate a block of HTML code that you can insert into each page of your Web site. This code will report information about the visitors who view your site, and you can view this information from the dashboard provided for your account on **www.statcounter.com**.

It is important to insert the code into every page on your site, because StatCounter will not be able to access and compile information on Web pages that do not contain the code. This will cause you to miss valuable opportunities to analyze pages that may be underperforming or capitalize on pages that are performing well.

Here are some of the statistics and information you can view from your StatCounter dashboard:

Popular Pages

This feature will show you the pages of your Web site that are receiving the highest amount of visitor traffic. Ideally, your home page should receive the most traffic of any page of your Web site because you want visitors to see this page first. If another page on your site is receiving more traffic than your home page, you should analyze that page to see if it contains higher keyword density or has more inbound links than your home page.

You can also use the Popular Pages feature to determine which pages should contain CGI forms and direct links to the creative works you have for sale. You can capitalize on frequently visited pages to build your e-mail marketing lists and generate more robust sales by taking advantage of the traffic flow on these pages.

Entry and Exit Pages

This feature will tell you the first page visitors see when they arrive at your Web site and the last page they view before they leave your site. This will tell you which page is the most common entry point for your Web site visitors and give you an idea of how visitors navigate your Web site. If a Web page other than your order page is the most common exit point, you may want to analyze that page to see if the content is confusing or if it contains content that is not appealing to your Web site visitors.

Came From

StatCounter offers the "came from" feature to help you determine where visitors to your site have been immediately before navigating to your site. This will tell you how many people find your site via a search engine and which search engine they are using. It will also tell you how well the inbound links that you or another Web site owner have placed on another Web site are performing — if an inbound link is performing well, you may want to consider ways to generate more traffic for the Web page containing that link so you can drive more traffic to your Web site.

Keyword Analysis

This tool tells you what keywords search engine users are using to find pages on your Web site. A keyword that generates a high volume of traffic is a good tool for your Web site, and you can capitalize on this by increasing the keyword density of that word or phrase in your Web site content.

If you have targeted a keyword in your content that is generating little traffic for your Web site, it may mean few visitors are searching for that word or phrase or there is a high volume of other Web sites using the same keywords. You may want to target a different keyword in your content or try increasing the density of that keyword in your content to see if its performance improves.

Visit Length

This feature tells you how long visitors stay on each page of your Web site. If a page on your site has a long average visit length, it is a good indication that visitors are interested in the content contained on that page. This is a good page to use to promote your creative works or build your e-mail marketing list.

If a particular page has a short average visit length, it could mean visitors to that Web page find the material on that page confusing, or they may not consider the content relevant to their needs. It is a good idea to analyze that page to see if the content needs to be improved. If the page is not relevant to your visitors' needs and interests, you may want to consider deleting the page altogether.

Returning Visitors

This tool will tell you how many visitors have returned to each page on your site. If your home page has a high number of repeat visitors, it means your Web site content is effective and visitors are interested in your creative works. If another page has many repeat visitors, you will know the content on that Web page is strong and visitors are likely bookmarking that page in their favorites lists.

If you are using e-mail marketing to build your online art business, use a page with frequent repeat visitors to build your subscriber base by placing a CGI form on that page.

Country, State, City, ISP

StatCounter offers this feature to tell you where your visitors live or work. If you find a high percentage of visitors live in a certain geographic area, then you may want to consider submitting your Web site to a local search engine that serves that area or using means of marketing locally to residents of that area. It may be that people in certain geographic areas are particularly receptive to your creative works, and this StatCounter feature gives you the ability to identify and capitalize on this.

When used in combination, these tools can provide a wealth of information that you can use to fine-tune your online business so you can sell more creative works and generate more profit.

OneStatFree

Another free Web site traffic analysis tool is available at **www. onestatfree.com**. Like StatCounter, OneStatFree offers quick registration and a simple HTML block to place within your Web pages. It also offers most of the same analysis tools as StatCounter, but it includes some extra tools that may be useful when you are analyzing your Web site's traffic:

Time Analysis

OneStatFree offers a feature that can tell you which hours of the day, which days of the week, which weeks of the month, and which months of the year each page receives the most traffic. Although the time of day when most visitors view your site may not be particularly important to you unless you plan to run a two-hour sale on some of your creative works, knowing which days and months your Web pages receive the most traffic can be useful for timing autoresponder messages and announcing sales and promotions. You can also adjust your pricing structure to charge premium prices during months when the site is most active and discounted prices during the slow months.

Web Site Comparison

OneStatFree divides registered Web sites into numerous categories, such as Arts, Business, Health and Fitness, and Web logs. You can use the comparison tool to see how well your Web site fares in search engine rankings and other statistics, as compared to other sites in your chosen category.

This can be a particularly useful tool for improving your Web site's content, because you can easily identify Web sites that are performing better than yours. Then, you can visit those sites to analyze their content so you can gather ideas for improving the content of your own Web site.

OneStatFree features a chart on its home page that lists all the Web site categories available — visitors of **www.onestatfree.com** can view the rankings for each category, regardless of whether they have registered accounts. This can help drive traffic to your Web site, because each of the rankings contains links to the sites that are being compared.

Whether you use StatCounter or OneStatFree is a matter of personal preference. As noted in this section, OneStatFree offers additional tools for analyzing your Web site's traffic and performance, but this site is also more heavily focused on promoting its premium products, such as OneStat Web Site Analytics ($125), which provides an even greater level of detailed site analysis, and RankStat SEO Tools ($191), which assists Web site owners with tailoring content to improve search engine rankings.

There are also a number of paid visitor tracking tools available, such as those offered at **www.metasun.com**, which can track additional statistics such as sales conversion percentages, number of file downloads, and specific visitor demographics. If you want to obtain a large amount of information about your visitors and their activities on your Web site, you can purchase Metatracker for $50 for one Web site or $125 for up to five Web sites.

Accounting, Business, and Financial Tools

As you have learned throughout this book establishing and running an art-related business online takes more than just superior artistic ability — it also takes a high level of business savvy. There are several tools available that can help you manage the business side of your online art venture and make your business more profitable.

Accounting and Financial Tools

One of the crucial elements of building a successful business is the ability to effectively manage your business's money. Profitable businesses have to account for marketing, inventory, materials, and other expenses while pricing products to provide revenue over and above these expenses.

These tools can help you manage your business's finances so you can reduce expenses and maximize profit.

Microsoft Money

Microsoft Money is a software application that can help you manage and track your finances all in one place. You can purchase Microsoft Money Plus Home and Business at **www.microsoft. com/money** for $89.99; however, Microsoft frequently offers a $30 mail-in rebate, so you can obtain this software for a final price of $59.99. You can also download a free 60-day trial of this software from the same Web site so you can familiarize yourself with the features before you purchase it.

Microsoft Money Plus Home and Business gives you basic features available in many software packages, such as checkbook balancing, spending categorization, and budget creation. It also allows you to prepare for tax season and manage your investments, such as IRA contributions, stocks, and money market accounts.

You can download transactions from most major financial institutions to Microsoft Money Home and Business, so you will not have to manually update your accounts when you log in to the software program.

It also gives you a number of business tools to help you manage your business, such as invoice creation, compilation of business reports, payroll management, and invoice and receivables monitoring.

Quicken

Quicken is another financial management software tool you can use to make sure your business stays profitable. At $59.99, it is somewhat less expensive than Microsoft Money Home and Business, although it lacks a number of the business features of Microsoft Money.

Specifically, the current version of Quicken does not give you the ability to create business reports or invoices and does not allow you to manage payroll tasks online. If these functions are not important to you, Quicken will easily handle most of the other elements required to keep your creative business financially sound.

You can purchase Quicken 2008 at **http://quicken.intuit.com;** however, the Web site does not currently offer a free trial version of the software, so you will not be able to test its features before you make a purchase.

GnuCash

GnuCash is a free alternative to Microsoft Money Home and Business and Quicken. When you download the software from **www.gnucash.org,** you will have access to a number of tools that will allow you to effectively manage your personal and business finances.

GnuCash allows you to set up multiple accounts, so you can manage your personal checking, savings, business, and investment accounts from one dashboard. You can set up accounts payable to manage your expenditures for supplies and marketing expenses, liability accounts to handle your personal and business loans, and credit card accounts to keep track of your unsecured debt.

You can also use GnuCash to manage payroll tasks, create customer invoices, manage customer and vendor data, and keep track of tax and billing terms for your customers.

This software application features frequent updates, so you will not have to worry about your software becoming obsolete.

Like Microsoft Money Home and Business and Quicken, GnuCash gives you the ability to download transactions from the Web sites of major financial institutions so updating your accounts is an effortless process.

With a variety of functions and features, GnuCash can be an excellent financial management solution if you do not want to invest your money in a paid financial software package.

Business Tools

You can also use tools that will help you create a business plan. Many online businesspeople do not believe they need to create a business plan, particularly if they do not have employees or investors; however, a business plan is essential if you want to plan for the future growth and success of your business. A business plan is also necessary if you decide to pursue a loan to finance future expansion of your business.

Creating a business plan can seem like a daunting task if you have never undertaken the endeavor of creating one for a business. Fortunately, you can access resources that will provide you with sample plans for a variety of business types and give you templates you can use to create your own business plan.

BPlans

You can access more than 500 sample business plans at **www.bplans.com**. These plans represent a wide variety of business plan styles and provide samples of plans for various industries.

Viewing sample business plans can be a great exercise before you create your own plan — you get to see how different businesses approach their plans and identify techniques that will be effective in your own business plan.

This Web site also contains many articles that cover different aspects of your plan, giving you advice about what types of information to include and how to present the information so that your business vision will be communicated clearly and effectively to potential investors, loan officers, and other people who will have the power to influence the success of your business and help you reach your financial and career goals.

You can also access several calculators that will help you create a realistic road map for your business — you can use these tools to calculate startup costs, determine when your business will break even, and even determine the return on investment you can expect from paid advertising efforts such as pay-per-click marketing.

Business Plan Pro

If you need additional assistance to create a business plan, you may consider purchasing Business Plan Pro. This software includes more than 500 business plan samples and gives you a number of templates to build your own plan. Using this software gives you step-by-step assistance in creating a business plan, so you can make sure all elements of your business are considered and included in your final business plan document.

You can also import data from Excel spreadsheets or Quicken to streamline the financial analysis portion of the plan. This feature will save you hours of time that you would otherwise spend transferring numbers and statistics from another document to your business plan.

Business Plan Pro is available at **www.bplans.com/mk/bpp_ jp.cfm** for $99.95.

The tools described in this chapter can be valuable in getting your creative business started and achieving success once your business is up and running. Now let us move on to another strategy for building your customer base and selling more creative works: social marketing.

Using Online Social Marketing to Build Your Clientele

If you have followed all the steps listed so far for setting up your online business, you have undoubtedly built an effective marketing system to get the word out abut your creative works. You may have even begun making some sales.

Chapters 9 and 10 will give you more tips and techniques for driving traffic to your Web site and generating interest for your creative works. These chapters contain information on strategies that are infrequently used by creative people selling their works online, so by adding these techniques to your marketing efforts, you will gain a significant advantage over most of the artists on the Internet today.

In this chapter, you will learn about the power of social marketing to gain visibility and drive traffic to your Web site.

What is Social Marketing?

In standard usage, social marketing refers to marketing that is designed to promote the common good of a community or group, rather than to promote a product or service. If you have seen anti-tobacco commercials on television or heard them on your favorite radio station, then you have witnessed social marketing at work.

On the Internet, social marketing takes on a somewhat different meaning. When you are using social marketing online, your primary strategy is to use venues that allow you to benefit others by educating, enlightening, or entertaining others. Your art becomes a secondary focus. The concept behind social marketing is that by building an online presence in social venues, you will gain the personal interest of others, and they will naturally want to find out more about you and your art.

Here are some ways you can use social marketing to take a less-aggressive approach to building your business.

MySpace

Using MySpace can be an excellent way to launch your social marketing efforts. There are millions of users on MySpace — many people use the Web site for personal pages, but a large number of entrepreneurs are also starting to use MySpace as a social marketing tool to reach a wide Internet audience.

Signing up for a MySpace account is simple. Just visit **www. myspace.com**, click the Sign Up button, and then fill in your contact information. In a matter of minutes, you will have your own MySpace page where you can create a personal profile; post blog entries; provide information about your interests and personal favorite things such as television shows, movies, and music; and even post videos and song files.

Once you have created your MySpace page, you can search for and join groups related to your personal art style or medium. By joining MySpace groups, you will build a network of people that you can share ideas with, refer clients to, or just keep in touch with to raise visibility for your Web site and your business.

You can also post photos of your creative works on MySpace. You will not be able to sell your works directly from your MySpace page, but you can use these photos to get people interested in your art so that they will want to visit your Web site to see more of your works or purchase them for their homes and offices.

If you are a musician who wants to sell your songs online, you can sign up for a MySpace Music Artist account so you can upload and post some of the songs you have created and post them on your MySpace page. To sign up for a Music Artist account, click the Music tab along the top bar of the MySpace home page, then click the Artist Signup Link on the next page. You will then fill in your contact information, your band name (if you have one), and the genre of your music. MySpace Music Artist accounts are free for musicians and will allow you to upload four songs to your page.

Uploading songs to your Music Artist page is a way to let visitors listen to your songs so they will want to visit your Web site to purchase your music. Visitors will not be able to download the songs on your MySpace page, so you will not have to worry about theft of your music.

Discussion Board Postings

Another good way to use social marketing to build your business is by participating in discussion boards. Discussion boards are a place where Internet users can have asynchronous conversations that may last hours or even days. The discussion is moved forward when each person posts a message relating to the previous message or to the topic that is being discussed. Groups of related posts are organized in threads, which show the chronology of the discussion from the beginning post that initiated the discussion to the most recent post. Discussion board threads continue until the original topic has been thoroughly discussed or until the participants tire of the discussion and move on to another topic.

A discussion board may have threads on several topics at once — larger discussion boards with many active participants may have hundreds of active threads being updated with new posts.

Most discussion boards follow a theme — there are discussion boards for people to discuss a wide range of interests, from art, to music, to food, to nearly any other topic you could imagine. This allows people with common interests to gather for networking, idea sharing, or just idle chatter.

You can find message boards in a couple of different ways. First, you can use a message board directory to find boards related to your particular interest. There are numerous message board directories that list thousands of boards for you to choose from. One of the largest directories is **www.big-boards.com**, which lists more than 2,000 discussion boards, categorized according to a number of topics. There is an entire section dedicated to art-related topics — you can browse the discussion boards in this section to find people with the same creative interests as you.

Another good discussion board directory is Yahoo! Message Boards, available at **http://messages.yahoo.com.** This Web site contains links to hundreds of message boards on a wide variety of topics. You can find discussion boards focused on fine arts, crafts, music, and photography, so no matter what type of creative works you sell, you can find people with similar interests.

The second way to find discussion boards is to check art-related Web sites that you may use anyway. Many discussion boards are part of Web sites — the Web site owners use the discussion boards to increase traffic to their sites so they can promote their products and services to discussion board members.

The discussion board at **www.wetcanvas.com** is one example of an art-related board that is part of a larger Web site. The Web site home page provides links to articles about various topics of interest to artists and to contests that creative people can enter to gain exposure and win cash prizes. The discussion board that is part of this Web site has hundreds of members and contains discussions on topics such as art techniques, what kinds of materials artists use, and how they sell their art online.

It also contains a number of topics only loosely related to art (and some not related to art), so members can have discussions about random topics while they are taking a break from their creative works.

The WetCanvas message board is a particularly useful tool for artists and other creative people because its members tend to be serious about promoting art online and about helping fellow creative people to reach success on the Internet.

Another popular discussion board is available at **www.ebsqart. com**. You may register on this discussion board either as a patron or as an artist. To register as an artist, you will need to become a member of EBSQ. You can apply for a membership by visiting the membership link on the Web site's home page. On the EBSQ discussion board, you will find many artists who are serious about establishing a profitable business online and many patrons who are interested in supporting and promoting the careers of working artists.

If you sell a portion of your creative works on eBay, or you are thinking about offering some of your works for sale on eBay (more on this in Chapter 11), another good resource is the collection of discussion boards available on **www.ebay.com**. There are several art-related discussion boards and even a board just for artists that allows people like you to discuss the ins and outs of selling creative works on eBay. This can be a valuable resource for you, because you can learn from the trials and the mistakes that other artists have made when building their art businesses.

Promoting Your Works through Discussion Boards

As with any type of social marketing, the key to successful marketing on discussion boards lies in taking a somewhat passive approach, rather than putting your business front and center. You will want to build online relationships through your discussion board postings, rather than just showing up and promoting your art to a group of people who do not know you.

When you find a discussion board that matches your interests, the first thing you should do after you register is to look for a "new members" section. This section may contain threads that will give you information on the board's terms of use — what you may and may not post on the discussion board and in which sections you can post certain types of content. It is important to read through these threads before you submit your first post to the discussion board. Posting inappropriate content or material that violates the discussion board's terms of use can cause you to be banned from the discussion board quickly. Even if you are not banned from the board, you are not likely to make many friends this way.

Respecting a discussion board's terms of use and rules of etiquette will go a long way toward helping you establishing online relationships that can advance your creative career.

After you have read through the terms of use and etiquette threads, you are ready to begin posting messages on the discussion board. You will want to start with the board's "Introduce Yourself" thread. This is a good place to tell members about your background and interests and give some information about the types of art you like to create. It is also a good place to start building relationships with members of the board. Make sure your introductory post is colorful and interesting. Tell members things about your life that are unique without boasting or giving the impression that you think you are special so you will get many responses from members, welcoming you to the board.

Here is an example of a good introductory post that will make members want to know more about you and the works you create:

Hi everybody! I'm Joe Smith, an abstract painter from Las Vegas, Nevada. I enjoy going out into the desert and creating abstract paintings based on the shapes and colors of the mountains at sunset. I grew up in Las Vegas, so I've always been fascinated by the desert, especially at dusk. The feeling of being utterly alone in a vast expanse of sand and rock unlocks my creativity like nothing else.

One of my favorite things to do when I'm not painting is to take some of my works down to the Strip and ask people what they think the works represent. It's amazing what people see in abstract art — the human mind always seems to try to make sense of the unknown, so people see all kinds of images in my paintings, from animals to landscapes to, well… slot machines. It is Vegas, after all.

I live with my two cats, Nitro and Osiris, and my gecko, Sam. I look forward to meeting and getting to know all of you here!

Of course, you should include only information that is true. Do not introduce yourself on a message board by telling members you like to paint while skydiving — unless, of course, you can mix paints while hanging from an open parachute in mid-air. Internet users tend to be an incredulous lot, so if you make up information about yourself, most people will see right through it. This will ruin your credibility and your chances of using a discussion board to promote your business.

After you have submitted an introductory post, get involved in some of the other discussions currently developing on the board. In addition to posting your opinions and sharing your knowledge, let other members know you are reading their posts by replying with posts that comment on their insights, ask for elaboration, or otherwise reference their posts. People like to talk about themselves and will feel more connected to you if they know you are interested in their opinions and insights.

Over time, you will develop close relationships with some of the other board members, and you will find these members will be more than willing to help you promote your business by letting friends, family, and business associates know about your art. No artist can create works that everyone will like and appreciate, so when other board members find a potential client who is looking for a style or type of creative work that they do not provide, they will be glad to refer those people to you.

Likewise, if you create abstract paintings and you meet a potential client who is looking for bronze sculpture, do not hesitate to refer that person to a discussion board member that creates art from bronze. Helping out other creative business owners will go a long way toward establishing relationships with them so they will be more inclined to send you business as well.

Here is one point to keep in mind when you are writing discussion board posts — most discussion boards do not allow members to link to their Web sites in posts. This keeps people from joining boards for the sole purpose of posting advertisements. No one wants to participate in a discussion that is littered with advertisements, so board moderators enforce this rule by deleting posts that contain obvious advertisements and sometimes even banning the members who submit these posts. Regardless of whether a particular message board has this rule, it is a good idea to refrain from including links to your Web site — it makes other board members less likely to want to interact with you, because they feel like you are just there to try to sell your products.

Some discussion boards may have sections or subsections where this rule does not apply. If this is the case, these sections will be clearly marked and may contain terms of use or rules of etiquette that are separate from those governing use of the rest of the board. You can use these sections to advertise your Web site, your blog, or any other marketing site or page you have built to promote your creative works.

Using Your Profile and Signature to Drive Traffic

You may wonder how people on discussion boards will be able to find your Web site if you do not specifically talk about your business in discussion board posts. There are two primary ways of accomplishing this — by providing your Web site link in your personal profile and by linking to your Web site in your signature.

When you register on a discussion board, you will have the opportunity to build a personal profile. This may include a photograph or image, your name, your location, your blog and Web site addresses, and other information you provide.

As you build relationships on discussion boards, other members who read your posts will visit your profile to learn more about you. From there, they can click the links to visit your Web site, blog, or other promotional page.

You will also have the opportunity to write a custom signature, which will appear beneath each of your discussion board posts. Most discussion boards allow Web site links in signatures, so people reading your posts can immediately visit your site or blog.

When writing your signature, make sure to review the site's terms of use to find out how many links you can include — some discussion boards limit you to two or three links. If you have more than three blogs or Web sites, provide links to your most effective ones in your signature, and make sure you prominently place links to your other Web sites and blogs on the ones your signature links to.

Facebook

Facebook is another excellent tool for social marketing. It allows you to make your online presence known without aggressive advertising and places advertisements in a social context to make your ads seem more like suggestions from friends.

You can create a free Facebook page by going to **www.facebook.com** and clicking the Sign Up button. Fill out your contact information, and you will be on your way to creating a profile page that others can use to find you.

With a free Facebook page, you can upload a personal photo as well as add details to your profile such as your location, your personal interests and preferences, and your Web site and blog addresses. If you have an e-mail account through Gmail, Facebook can also automatically notify people on your e-mail contact list that you have a new Facebook page ready for viewing.

Having a Facebook page can be a good way for people with whom you have lost touch to find you. This includes people you went to school with or previously worked with, as well as previous clients and potential clients who have lost your contact information.

Facebook also offers business solutions called Social Ads that combine elements of social marketing and pay-per-click marketing. With Social Ads, you write an ad just as you would for a pay-per-click marketing campaign. However, instead of having the ad shown to everyone who uses a particular search term, the ad is placed in the context of a Facebook user's interaction on your Web site or Facebook page.

Information about how Facebook users interact on your Web site is obtained by another product Facebook offers called Beacon. Beacon consists of a few lines of code that you place on your business Web pages — this code allows Facebook to gather information on your Web site visitors who take specific actions on your site and create short stories on their own Facebook pages about those transactions.

Your Social Ads copy will appear in the context of these stories. Here is how a Social Ad may appear on a Facebook user's page:

Jan recently purchased the artwork "Doves in Flight" From Joe Smith's Art Studio.

Joe Smith's Art Studio
Expressive, colorful paintings to bring life to your walls!
Buy today; have your art shipped tomorrow!

Social Ads work because they use the power of social influence — if a person visits a friend's Facebook page and learns he or she has purchased an artwork from you, that person will be more likely to visit your Web site and purchase an artwork for his or her own home or office. People want to buy from businesses and people their friends have bought from, and Facebook Social Ads allow you to take advantage of this by integrating your ads into a social context.

Now let us move on to another way you can build a solid client base — e-mail and newsletter marketing.

E-mail & Newsletter Marketing

In Chapter 8, you learned about using autoresponder services to create opt-in forms for your Web site and manage e-mail messages to people who subscribe to your e-mail list. This chapter will tell you how you can use e-mail marketing to build a base of loyal clients who will frequently check your Web site for new creative works and refer their family and friends to you for commissioned works.

Why Does E-mail Marketing Work?

Imagine that during your day you run across a Web site that contains products that interest you. You start to think about how these products could be beneficial for you, and you consider purchasing one or more of the products for your own use. Then, something else distracts you, and you close your Web browser, intending to come back to it later. As new tasks come along, your attention is taken further away from the Web site you visited, and eventually, you forget about the items you wanted to purchase.

Unfortunately for Internet marketers, this is a scenario that happens all too often. No matter how well you have designed your Web site or how tempting your product selection is, you are competing with all the other things that vie for your visitors' attention. You will lose customers far more frequently to the distractions in your visitors' lives than to other Internet marketers that are competing for your business.

If you give your visitors the opportunity to subscribe to your e-mail marketing list, you will be able to frequently remind them of your products so that when they find a time free from distractions, they will be able to return to your Web site and purchase your creative works.

E-mail marketing also works because it gives you the opportunity to provide subscribers with relevant, useful information that will give them an educational and entertaining break from their day-to-day tasks. It also establishes you as an authority in your field, because you will be the one who will provide information that is readily visible to your subscribers — by sending frequent e-mails about your products and different art-related topics, your subscribers will come to trust you as an expert on your own particular style of art, even if there are other artists who are more knowledgeable about art-related topics than you.

Finally, e-mail marketing works because your subscribers can feel special when they receive special promotional offers and discounts from you that you do not offer to other visitors that view your Web site. They can be the first to know about new artworks you have completed, and you can even tell them about special creative works and projects that are not available to the public. By giving your subscribers a sense of exclusivity, you will build a loyal client base who will buy from you time and time again.

Types of E-mail Campaigns

Once you have used opt-in forms to build a base of e-mail subscribers, there are several ways you can use e-mail campaigns to stay in front of your subscribers and continue to build interest for your creative works. Different types of e-mail campaigns use different approaches to gain reader interest, but they all ultimately lead to one singular purpose — the sale of your creative works.

E-mail Mini Courses

Creating an e-mail mini course is an excellent way to remind your subscribers about your business, because you can spend a few hours creating a course and put it to work for you for years to come.

As a creative person, what knowledge could you share through an e-mail course that would benefit your subscribers? No matter what types of creative works you are selling, you have special knowledge that could benefit your readers. For example, if you are a visual artist — say, a landscape painter — you could easily create an e-mail course instructing subscribers on how to correctly hang and display paintings. If you have been in the art business for a while, or if you obtained a college degree in art, this topic may seem like second nature to you. To your readers, however, it may be a source of significant confusion and frustration. They may not know anything about how to correctly hang a painting, how high to hang a particular piece, or how far apart to hang artworks to create a visually pleasing environment.

If you are not convinced, ask your spouse, your grandmother, and your boss how they think a person should correctly hang paintings. At least two out of the three people will have no idea how to hang paintings correctly. Knowledge that is second nature to you is likely foreign to people who are not artists.

To get the maximum exposure from your e-mail mini course, divide the material you want to cover into several parts. Using the above example, you could come up with at least six parts for your "How to Hang and Display Paintings" e-mail course:

- Selecting Correctly Sized Artworks for Your Room

- Choosing Landscape- or Portrait-Oriented Paintings

- Selecting the Right Hanging Hardware for Your Art

- How to Install Hanging Hardware on Your Artworks

- Selecting the Correct Height for Your Paintings

⊛ Spacing Your Artworks Properly to Avoid the Sense of Clutter

You may be able to come up with more subtopics, but you may lose reader interest if you divide your e-mail course into more than six parts.

Once you have decided on your subtopics for your e-mail course, use your autoresponder service to draft e-mails that will contain the material covered in your course. Using the "How to Hang and Display Paintings" example, you would draft a total of eight e-mails — one introducing the subscriber to the course and telling him or her about what can be expected from the course, one for each of the six parts of the course, and one thanking the subscriber for reading the course and inviting him or her to visit your Web site or blog for more art-related information.

Your e-mails should be written in a conversational tone — you want your subscribers to be entertained as well as educated by your course, so you will want to keep it as light as possible. Do not make your readers feel as if they are reading a science textbook.

Each e-mail should include a short blurb containing your Web site address and an invitation to visit your online gallery. It does not have to be anything elaborate — it can be a simple line or two such as, "Joe Smith has been creating art and helping clients display their artworks for more than a decade. To find out more about Joe's artworks, visit www.joesmithartstudio.com."

Once you have written all the e-mails for your mini course, load them into your autoresponder, and set each e-mail to go out on a different day. Using the above example, you could send out the introductory e-mail as soon as a visitor subscribes to your e-mail list, and then send out one part of the e-mail course every two days. Your final e-mail could go out two days after the last part of the course.

By using an autoresponder service to do this, you do not have to worry about remembering to send out the parts of your e-mail course to subscribers at the appropriate times. Once you have set up your e-mails in the autoresponder, it will automatically send out each e-mail at the intervals you specify. This is a good way to promote your business without adding hours of work to your schedule each day.

How do e-mail courses help you promote your business? Statistics show that on average, you will need to make a contact with a potential client seven times before he or she makes a purchase. Of course, this is not going to be the case with every customer — some will decide to purchase one of your creative works on the first few visits, and others may read your e-mails for months before committing to a purchase. Still, e-mail courses are an easy way to make several contacts with your potential customers. As long as each e-mail contains relevant, useful information that your subscribers can apply to their lives, it will be as effective as if you had written a personal e-mail just for them.

If you have written more than one e-mail course, use your final e-mail to not only thank your subscribers for taking the course and to invite them to browse your gallery, but also to tell them about other free courses you offer. If a subscriber signs up for another course, you will have several more opportunities to contact the client and invite him or her to browse and purchase your creative works.

Broadcasts

Broadcast e-mails are another important element of your marketing. When you send out a broadcast e-mail, you are making contact with every one of your subscribers at once, regardless of when they subscribed. These e-mails can tell your subscribers about special promotions and discounts on your artwork, a new creative project or gallery showing, or enhancements or changes to your Web site.

To maximize the effectiveness of your broadcast e-mails, try to limit them to no more than one or two a week. It is important to stay in front of your customers and potential customers, but if they start seeing one or two e-mails every day from you, they will soon grow tired of being on your subscriber list. Keep in touch, but do not burn your subscribers out.

Newsletters

Newsletters are an excellent way to maintain contact with your subscribers without making them feel like you are trying to sell them something. Your newsletters can highlight a new series of artworks you have begun, tell your readers about a charity event to which you have donated creative works, or show images from a recent art gallery showing that featured your works. You can also use newsletters to provide informative articles that your readers can use when selecting and purchasing creative works.

Depending on the scale of your business, you may have enough material to send out a monthly newsletter. If not, a bimonthly or quarterly newsletter is fine. You should have enough material to keep your readers interested for a while and plenty of images to showcase your creative works.

When creating your newsletter, make sure the layout and color scheme match your Web site as closely as possible, and include your business logo if you have one. Doing this will help build branding — people will see your logo and your page layout and immediately know from whom the e-mail is being sent.

It is important to make your make your newsletters look as professional as possible. Even though you are using your newsletters to inform and entertain your readers, you are also building a professional image with these e-mails. A well-designed newsletter will show your subscribers that you area professional and that you take your business seriously.

Most autoresponders will let you set up and send HTML e-mails so that your newsletter can mirror the design of your Web site. However, not all e-mail applications can correctly display HTML e-mails, so it is a good idea to put the newsletter on your Web site and provide a link in your e-mail for people who cannot display HTML messages.

Sharing E-mail Addresses With Others

It can be tempting to share the e-mail addresses you gather through your marketing efforts, either for profit or to join forces with another artist so you can both have larger subscriber lists. However, this is a bad idea and can cause significant damage to your reputation and your business.

First, selling or otherwise giving the e-mail addresses of your subscribers to someone else without their express consent violates federal privacy laws and can cause you to incur stiff fines or even time in prison.

Second, it erodes the trust of your customers. No one wants to receive scores of e-mails from people they do not know because you sold or gave away their e-mail address. Once you sell or give away an address, you have no control over how another person chooses to use it.

Now let us move on to learning how to use eBay auctions to sell a portion of your artworks, handmade crafts, music recordings, or photographs.

Using eBay Auctions to Promote & Sell Your Art

So far, this book has explored many ways you can use your business Web site, blog, and other promotional tools to gain visibility for your art and generate sales through your Web site. In this chapter, you will learn about using eBay auctions to generate additional sales, as well as increase traffic to your Web site.

Why Sell on eBay?

EBay was probably not the first promotional vehicle you thought of when you initially contemplated selling your creative works online. To many people, eBay is simply a huge online garage sale where people auction off unwanted merchandise and household goods for a fraction of their retail value. Since its early days, eBay has been a repository for cheap merchandise, which has done little to improve its image in the online marketplace.

When it comes to vintage catsup bottles, used iPods, and moon-faced Hummel figurines of questionable origin, people who visit eBay are looking for a bargain. When it comes to original artwork, however, there is a large pool of buyers who are looking to purchase art at reasonable prices but do not expect to be able to obtain quality works for only a few dollars.

EBay serves as an excellent resource for working artists. Hundreds of creative people are able to earn a comfortable living from eBay sales alone, and thousands more use eBay auctions to augment their gallery and Web site sales.

One of the best reasons to sell a portion of your creative works on eBay is because this Web site receives hundreds of thousands of visitors each day. When you post a featured auction listing to sell one of your artworks on eBay, it is not uncommon for your auction to receive 200 or more visits in a week. Getting enough traffic to your Web site to have even half that many people look at one particular artwork would take enormous time and effort.

Thousands of artworks sell on eBay every week for prices that are acceptable to both working artists and consumers. It is not clear why homeowners, doctors, lawyers, and corporate interior decorators scour eBay for original art, but they do. Maybe it is because they do not want the stress of wading through hundreds of artist Web sites to find the perfect artwork. Maybe it is because they perceive original artwork as costing thousands of dollars, and they are looking only to spend a few hundred dollars. Maybe it is because they have heard that eBay is a fantastic place to find art. Whatever the reason, their presence on eBay is a good opportunity for you to introduce yourself as a creative professional and sell some art in the process.

Another good reason to sell on eBay is you can sell creative works much more quickly than on your Web site or through a physical gallery. You do not have to wait for months for someone to come along and find your artwork; instead, you can create a work and have it sold and shipped to a buyer within a matter of days. Some artists who sell their works through auction listings are able to sell works as fast as they create them, which generates a constant source of revenue that traditional gallery artists are not able to enjoy.

How much can you make selling art on eBay? With the exception of those people who list their artworks for $1 each (more on that later), art on eBay frequently sells from $40 to $700 per work. There are a number of artists who make six-figure salaries by selling art on eBay and many others who have replaced their "day job" salaries with the income made from eBay sales.

Selling your creative works on eBay takes a significant amount of work, patience, creativity, and determination. As with any online marketing tool, you need to know and use specific strategies to successfully compete with the thousands of other artists, crafters, musicians, and photographers selling their works. After all, at any given time, there are about 12,000 original artworks for sale in the "Self-Representing Artists" category alone and many other creative works for sale in other categories. Although that may sound daunting, selling art this way is like most other online ventures — 10 percent of the suppliers make 90 percent of the money. So how do you get in that 10 percent?

Fortunately, most people who post auctions on eBay do not have the marketing knowledge to succeed with auction sales. Many artists who decide to try selling creative works on eBay assume that if they take five minutes to upload a photo of the artwork into an auction template, give it a catchy title, and post it for the world to see, people will flock to bid on the artwork.

In the early days of eBay, when few artists were selling original works through online auctions, little sophistication was necessary to successfully sell arts and crafts. Now, there is too much competition to rely on this kind of "build it and they will come" mentality.

Getting visitors to view your auction listings and bid on your artworks is less about creating art and more about crafting auction listings. Fortunately, this is not terribly difficult, but it requires knowing a bit about how auctions work in eBay's most competitive categories, which includes art-related categories. In the following pages, you will learn how to craft auction listings that attract visitors, capture interest, and compel visitors to bid on your artwork.

Setting Up Your eBay Account

Setting up an eBay account so you can post auctions to sell your creative works is a fairly simple process. You will need to set up both a buyer's account and a seller's account to post auction listings. Go to **www.ebay.com** and click on the "Register" link to begin setting up your account.

To create a basic buyer's account, you will need to enter your contact information and your date of birth and select a username for your account. Your username should reflect your business and can be the same as your Web site address.

After you have registered with eBay, you can create a seller's account by logging in to eBay and clicking the "Sellers" link on your My eBay page.

To create a seller's account, you will need to provide eBay with a credit card so you can be charged for seller's fees you incur from posting auction listings and selling your creative works. If you have a PayPal account, you can elect to have your seller's fees deducted from PayPal, but you will still need to provide a credit card as a backup.

Fees for Selling An Item

You will incur fees for each item that you list in an eBay auction. Auction fees can be quite substantial, so it is important to know how much you will be charged so you can correctly price your item to make a profit.

Here is a listing of the fees that you may incur when placing auction listings on eBay:

Listing Fees

Regardless of whether your item sells, you will be charged a listing fee every time you place an item for sale in an eBay auction. The amount of the listing fee depends on the starting price you list when your auction launches. The greater your starting price for an item, the higher the listing fee will be. Here are the current listing fees charges by eBay:

AUCTION STARTING PRICE	LISTING FEE
$0.01 to $0.99	$0.20
$1 to $9.99	$0.40
$10 to $24.99	$0.60
$25 to $49.99	$1.20
$50 to $199.99	$2.40
$200 to $499.99	$3.60
Over $500	$4.80

Final Value Fees

Final value fees are charged in addition to listing fees if your item sells. Final value fees are based on the amount your item sells for at the end of the auction. Here are the final value fees currently charged by eBay:

CLOSING PRICE FOR YOUR ITEM	FINAL VALUE FEE
Item Not Sold	No final value fee
$0.01 to $25	5.25 percent of closing price
$25.01 to $1,000	5.25 percent of the first $25, then 3.25 percent of the closing price above $25
$1000.01 or more	5.25 percent of the first $25, 3.25 percent of the next $975, then 1.5 percent of the closing price over $1,000

Again, final value fees are in addition to listing fees — they do not replace listing fees if your item sells.

Reserve Fees

If you want to make sure you get a good price for your creative work, you can place a reserve on your auction selling price. A reserve is a minimum price below which you are not obligated to sell your item to the highest bidder. If the highest bid price for your item does not meet the reserve you have set, the highest bidder will not be entitled to your artwork.

You will still be charged listing fees for your auction, but setting a reserve can still be an effective way of making sure you do not sell your item for less than you spent creating and listing it.

If the highest bid does exceed the reserve you have set, you will be obligated to sell the item to the highest bidder. In this case, the reserve fees will be deducted from your total seller's fees for that auction.

Here are the reserve fees currently charged by eBay. They are based on the dollar amount of the reserve you have set:

RESERVE PRICE	RESERVE FEE
$0.01 to $49.99	$1
$50 to $199.99	$2
$200 and above	1 percent of the reserve price, subject to maximum reserve fee of $50

Buy it Now Fees

If you want to give your bidders the option to end the auction early by purchasing your artwork at a specific price, you can set a Buy it Now price for your auction. If you know you will have several bidders competing to win your auction, Buy it Now is a good tool to give someone the chance to buy your creative work at your optimal price. Here are the fees eBay currently charges for the Buy it Now option:

BUY IT NOW PRICE	BUY IT NOW FEE
$0.01 to $9.99	$0.05
$10 to $24.99	$0.10
$25 to $49.99	$0.20
$50 or more	$0.25

There are a number of other enhancements you can add to your auction listings — you can add a colored background or a border in the listing results to make your auction stand out, or place your auction in the "Featured Auctions" listings, which places your auction in front of all the standard listings so yours will be among the first auctions seen when a user searches your category.

EBay charges for each of these features, so take time to determine how much you can spend on a listing and still have a good chance of making a profit from your auctions. It is easy for artists to want to take advantage of every feature possible to gain the most exposure, but if you end up spending $40 in listing, final value, and enhancement fees, it may be difficult for you to realize a profit, particularly when you are just starting out with online auctions and are not well known in the eBay community.

Building Auction Listings

Once you have created your seller's account, you are ready to start posting auction listings to sell your creative works. To begin building an auction listing, place your pointer over the "Sell" link at the top of your account page, and select "Sell an Item" from the drop-down menu.

You will then select the category and subcategory in which you would like your auction listing to appear. One of the most popular categories for artists and other creative people is "Self-Representing Artists." This is a good category if you are selling visual artworks such as paintings, sculptures, or photographs, because eBay buyers know they can find original art in this category, rather than reproductions. You can also concurrently place your listing in another category, such as "Contemporary Art," to gain even more exposure for your listings. Keep in mind, though, that if you concurrently list your item in two categories, eBay will charge you listing fees for each category, effectively doubling the amount you will pay for listing your auction on eBay.

Choosing the Length and Timing of Your Auctions

Before you compose an auction listing, you will need to decide some important things such as how long you want your auction to run and when you want it to end. Both factors can affect how many bids your auction receives and how high the final bid is.

EBay allows you to run an auction for one, three, five, seven, or ten days. The listing template defaults to seven days, but you can shorten or lengthen this time if you feel it will provide you with a competitive advantage.

Some artists choose one- or three-day listings to convey a sense of urgency among bidders. Bidders who view these listings know if they do not put in their bids right away and place the top bid they are willing to pay for an artwork, they will lose out on the chance to win the auction.

The Auction Title

The first and one of the most important things to consider is the auction title. When people search for an item on eBay, they use keywords to find what they are looking for, just like Internet users search for Web sites using keywords. EBay's search engine searches the titles and descriptions of every active auction to find those keywords and then provides a list of all auctions that contain them.

It is crucial to make sure you are using good keywords in your auction title. You have fewer than 100 characters available, so every single word must work to bring in traffic and catch the reader's attention.

Most artists do not understand how to effectively use the available space in auction listing titles. They think they need to use titles as an attention-grabbing tool but do not realize that words that are not relevant to searches are a waste of critical space. When people load titles with things such as "WOW," "L@@K," and "MUST SEE," you can be sure they are not thinking about how people are going to find their auction. By not making this common mistake, you can put yourself far ahead of most of the other artists on eBay.

Crafting titles with useful and searchable words is easy to do, if you take time to think about it from the buyer's perspective. Essentially, you just have to ask yourself what you would be looking for if you were searching eBay for an artwork to hang in your home or office, if you were envisioning a particular artwork.

Here is an example: Let us say you are selling a large abstract painting done in reds and earth tones. Now take a minute to imagine yourself as a homeowner whose wife is tired of having an empty white wall behind the sofa. You log in to eBay, and then what?

Most likely, you are going to browse for a bit in the Art category, become overwhelmed, and then type some words in the search box to narrow down the choices. The sofa is brown leather, so you want a painting that complements this. You are partial to abstract art, but you would rather have geometric shapes than drips and swirls. So your search may look something like: painting brown red abstract shapes.

Now, use this information to write your title. It is all right to ignore all the usual rules of grammar here — your title can just be a list of words or phrases. In addition to the other keywords, it is also a good idea to include the name of your gallery, your initials, or some other word to identify you. Once people start noticing you, they will use this to specifically search for your listings. Let us suppose your initials are A. E. R. — your title may end looking something like this:

"AER Original Abstract Painting Brown Red Earthtone Geometric Shapes"

Now you have a title that is descriptive, keyword searchable, and easily identifies you.

The Auction Design

The next step in creating a superior auction is the design of the auction listing itself. Many sellers simply use eBay's default auction template, which creates a uniform and rather boring layout.

You can use a number of auction template generators to add visual interest to your listings. A free and highly versatile auction template builder is available at **www.robshelp.com**. You can add multiple images, customize the layout of your auction listing, and select unique fonts for your listing text to make your auctions stand out from those of your competitors.

An auction template builder can help you easily add lots of things to make your listings stand out, like textured backgrounds, multiple photos of your art, and unique fonts. You are essentially creating a Web page out of your auction listing that will grab the buyer's attention and keep him or her focused on your listing.

Once they have created a design that is uniquely their own, most successful artists use the same design for every auction. This creates a sort of "branding" tool that lets buyers know whose art they are looking at before they read a word of the auction listing.

One note about creating complex listing designs, though: adding textured backgrounds, animated GIFs, and other flashy items slows down the speed at which your listing page loads, particularly for dial-up users. If you add so much of this that it takes your page 10 seconds to load, it is like a car salesperson walking up to a customer and standing there adjusting his tie for 10 seconds before ever saying anything. Your buyer will move on and find another artwork to purchase.

Photographing Your Artwork

Since a buyer cannot stand in front of your artwork and see its colors and textures, they have to rely on your photographs to convey these elements. Your images have to be clear, properly lit, and free of keystoning and other visual distortions so the buyers can closely approximate what your artworks will look like in their homes and offices. More is better when it comes to photos. Shooting the artwork from several angles and distances helps the buyer "see" your art's details, dimensions, and feel.

It is a good idea to set up a "staging" area where you photograph all your paintings or sculptures for your auctions. By doing this, you can set up your lighting and your tripod position a single time, which will provide you with consistent results and save a great deal of time photographing your images.

Ideally, the background on which you place your artworks should be flat black. This will reduce the amount of color distortion appearing in your photos. You can accomplish this either by painting a wall black or by stretching black fabric over a portion of a wall. I opted for the fabric, simply because if I ever decide to move my staging area, I will not face the difficult task of painting over a white wall.

When it comes to lighting, you should use soft white light sources on either side of the painting, set at 45-degree angles toward the painting. The light source on one side of the painting should be slightly closer to the painting than the light source on the other side. This will help eliminate glare and harsh shadows that can ruin your photos.

If you have it available, use the "optical zoom" feature to take close-up shots of your paintings. Some digital cameras are equipped only with digital zoom, which is fine for taking pictures of the new family car for Grandma but not so good for capturing fine details of your art. If digital zoom is all you have available, it is better to skip the close-up shots altogether.

Although it seems like a common-sense thing to bring up, always use a tripod. It is surprising how many artists have every other element covered for creating good photographs, and then the pictures come out blurred because they were not willing to spend $20 on a serviceable tripod. A good tripod can make all the difference between clear, professional-looking images and sloppy, fuzzy pictures.

Also, you will notice that some of the artworks you see have impossibly vivid colors that just seem to pop off the screen. Some artists try for months to create that sort of effect in their auction photos, but without image manipulation software such as Adobe® Photoshop® or Paint Shop Pro, it is difficult to create images that will pop out on a viewer's monitor. With digital image manipulation, after the photos are taken, the artists use the software to create the illusion that the artworks are somehow brighter and more colorful than they are. It seems to be a popular technique, although one has to wonder how many disappointed buyers there are who pulled a painting out of a package only to find that the colors of the artwork were not as brilliant as they were represented in the seller's auction listing images.

There is no clear consensus on the digital manipulation issue, so whether you choose to try it in your auction listing images is a matter of personal choice. If you want to try it, you may wish to download a free trial version of Photoshop® or Paint Shop Pro for experimenting with enhancing your auction images. If it helps your sales, then continue using this technique.

One last thought on photos: If you browse through eBay art auctions, you will notice that quite a few artists have photos in their listings of their artwork in rooms that look as if they came out of a furniture catalog. In the vast majority of cases, the "rooms" are indeed images lifted off other Web sites. The artworks are then cropped out of other photos and superimposed in the room. Supposedly, this gives the buyer a better idea of how an artwork will look in a living space.

It is not clear whether "staging" your artworks in this manner helps sales. Some successful eBay artists use this technique in every auction; others do not use it, and there are a number of artists who feel this is an unfair representation of their competitors' works and a somewhat unethical way to misrepresent their own wares. The only advice that can be given here is that if you feel you need to do this, try to refrain from using images from other Web sites — it is not uncommon for artists to run into copyright infringement issues as a result of using images without permission. Of course, if you are like most of us, you do not have a room that is straight out of Ikea (stage lighting and all), and it may be difficult to create the sort of pristine environment for your artwork without using a stock image.

The Auction Text

Auction text is an often ignored element of auction listings. Artists reason that their auctions are about images, so not much description is necessary.

The truth is that buyers not only want to see pictures of your art, they want to know about it. Take the time to describe the artwork. How big is it? What colors were used? Is it smooth and sleek, or is it heavily textured? You may assume buyers can see all these things in the auction photos, but differences in monitor settings and quality can hide or distort these details in even the best photos. Since you do not have any control over this, you need to provide these details in words as well as in pictures.

In addition, it is important to include information about what the artwork means to you. What inspired the work? What were you thinking when you created the art? Was there some unique experience that made you hopelessly, obsessively compelled to put your thoughts and emotions about the experience on canvas? Many artists take the perceived high road on this, rationalizing that art should be personal to its owner and that they should not taint a buyer's concept of what an artwork "means."

Although this is an understandable position, it may be completely wrong. Buyers feel like they have some sort of insider knowledge when they learn what an artwork means to the artist. It gives them a story to tell when dinner guests comment on your painting hanging in their dining room.

Your "About Me" Page

Here is where everything begins to fall together. Although an "About Me" page is not technically part of any one auction listing, it is a part of your profile that can be accessed from every listing that you post on eBay.

Your "About Me" page is a carte blanche area for you to say whatever you want about yourself, your art, and your vision. This includes not only text, but also photos of yourself hard at work in your studio, examples from your art portfolio, and information on how to contact you directly. Use this space to your fullest advantage by also including your artist's statement, some highlights of your career as an artist, and, most important, the link to your individual artist Web site.

Unfortunately, eBay does not allow you to link directly to your Web site from your auction listings. On your "About Me" page, though, it is permissible to include a link to your Web site. If a buyer likes your art and has learned a little about you through your listing text, he or she will visit your "About Me" page to find out more about you — why you became an artist, whether you accept commissions, and other information. Once a buyer is on your "About Me" page, it is likely that he or she will follow the link to your Web site to learn even more about you.

Also, do not forget to include your studio logo that you made when you were building your individual artist Web site.

Aside from the ability to post auctions and receive bids before the paint on your latest masterpiece is even dry, this is one of the most important reasons to sell on eBay. If you have taken the time to get visits to your auctions through well-crafted titles; created interest with a unique design, professional photos, and descriptive text; and hooked your readers with content-rich information on your "About Me" page, then you will receive traffic for your Web site that would be otherwise completely unattainable. It is good if a visitor bids on your eBay auction. But if he or she does not but ends up on your Web site, all you need to do is get an e-mail address (through a newsletter subscription form) and you will have a potential customer whom you can target for years to come.

Your Auction Price

One point that is a mystery to many artists new to selling on eBay is how to price auctions. This can be tricky, because how you initially price each action has a huge bearing on the final price your paintings sell for.

The typical logic dictates that your starting bid price should be the minimum amount of money that you would be comfortable selling your artwork for. In other words, what is the lowest price you would accept for an artwork and not feel ripped off? Of course, to determine this figure, you need to keep track of how much you spent on materials for a particular artwork, how many hours you spent creating it, and how much you are investing in eBay listing fees. To a certain degree, this has to be a business decision rather than an emotional decision — there are artists who are particularly attached to a work who try to sell it on eBay for $10,000 or more. The only thing that accomplishes is wasting eBay listing fees and giving all the other eBay artists a good laugh.

You will undoubtedly notice there are also quite a few listings that start out at a nominal bid (usually, $1). This is a popular tactic used by new auction marketers — they figure that the low starting price will entice bids, and once people start bidding, the listing will end up with a "bidding war" that will culminate in a high closing price.

Unfortunately, this rarely works anymore. The artists that can get away with this sort of thing are the ones who have already developed a following they can count on to bid no matter what they produce. It can take years to develop that kind of following, and unless you have this sort of loyal clientele, using this technique is not recommended. At best, you will have thought to put a "reserve" on the listing and you will end up wasting eBay listing fees. At worst, you will not have placed a "reserve," and you will end up giving away a valuable artwork for $1.

Many artists have tried the $1 trick with little success. For those people, the mainstay of selling art should be the traditional logic described at the beginning of this section. Once you have a good idea of what your total costs are going to be, how many hours you have put into a particular work of art, and how much profit you want to gain from it, then you will be able to begin correctly pricing your artworks to fall between what you wanted to sell them for and what the buyers are willing to pay.

This, of course, requires some trial and error. Over time, however, this is the most effective way to make a substantial income from your creative works while you are building your online presence.

Your eBay Store

In addition to auction listings, you can also sell creative works in your eBay store. An eBay store allows you to list hundreds of items for sale at once and categorize each item to help users find your store items. The fees for listing these items are much lower than the fees for launching auctions so you can make a greater profit from your eBay store items than through auction items.

A standard eBay store costs $9.99 per month, and you can list items for as little as $0.05 per month. This allows you to have 100 creative works for sale at the same time for only $20 per month — and as your works sell, you can use the available slots to sell new works without incurring additional cost. Of course, you will still be responsible for final value fees for works that you sell through your eBay store.

Your eBay store listings will show up in your active auctions, so if a visitor views an auction listing but wants a variation of that painting, he or she can view several of your other works on your auction page and visit your eBay store to see all the items you have for sale on eBay. This creates an effective cross-selling tool to help you sell more artworks and develop long-term relationships with your clients.

Now, let us move on to ways you can effectively promote and sell each of the four main types of creative works sold on the Internet — fine art, handmade crafts, music, and photographs.

12

Selling Your Art Online: Your Own Virtual Gallery

The Internet has become a vibrant marketplace for artists seeking to promote and sell their works of fine art. A decade ago, few people would have believed that artists could create financially successful business without contracting with a physical gallery. The people of the fine art world believed that the traditional method of selling through art galleries was the only viable way to be taken seriously as an artist and to build a loyal following of buyers.

Today, there are thousands of fine artists who have built successful businesses online without having ever displayed an artwork in a physical gallery. Fine art has become a valuable addition to the Internet, because users can browse and select artworks without the hassle of visiting a gallery, dealing with salespeople, and paying marked-up prices for original fine art.

The Internet has also leveled the field for artists by giving them the ability to control the display, marketing, and prices of their own creative works. They no longer have to rely on gallery owners to tell them what their artworks are worth or pay large commissions to galleries for the privilege of displaying their art. Artists are now able to control the business aspects of selling art and can build lucrative businesses with their own creativity and marketing efforts.

Like any business, selling art online takes a quite a bit of perseverance and ingenuity, along with a little luck. This chapter will give you some things to consider while you are building your business and promoting your fine art online.

Using Your Art to Create Your Online Identity

When you are choosing artworks to sell online, it is important to remember that every piece of fine art you display will become part of your online identity. Buyers will come to know you not only for your blog posts and articles, but also for the type of artwork you sell online.

For this reason, it is crucial that your online portfolio conveys a sense of continuity. Many online artists want to sell works that reflect a variety of genres and styles. Some do this because they want visitors to see they are versatile; others do this because they simply want to experiment with many types of art.

Although experimentation is crucial for an artist to continue to evolve, it is much easier to build a successful business if the artworks you display online share a connection. This is not to say that all your artworks need to look virtually the same, but they should share some common traits. For example, you may use the female human form as a common element of the works you place for sale. Your style may vary somewhat throughout your online portfolio, but the common theme of the human female form should carry through all your fine art.

Although it demonstrates versatility, displaying many different types of artwork on the same Web site without a common thread tends to confuse visitors. When viewing your works, they have difficulty understanding your artistic vision, and it becomes impossible for them to associate a particular style of art with your name.

Create continuity throughout your online galleries, and you will find it much easier to build a loyal customer base that will return to your Web site to purchase art from you time and time again.

Determining What Art Sells Online

Like any business owner, an artist must create works that are in demand to build a successful business. It is crucial to know what types of artworks will sell online, so you can focus your efforts on creating these types of works.

This may seem like a concept that will significantly hamper your creativity, but you can still use your creativity to create artworks that will be attractive to buyers. Landscapes, for example, tend to sell well online — you can create your own unique spin on landscape paintings by creating scenes that use bold, contrasting colors for your landscape elements instead of focusing on blending colors that accurately match trees, clouds, and mountains.

In Chapter 11, you learned about the thousands of artists currently selling their creative works on eBay. Whether you choose to offer your own artworks on eBay, browsing through the listings in the Self-Representing Artists category will give you a good sense of what is popular online right now.

As you browse through the listings, take note of which auctions end with respectable sales and which ones end with no bids. This will tell you quite a bit about the types of art that are in demand online, and it will also tell you which types of art to avoid. For example, you may find that paintings containing images of cats tend to do well, while abstract paintings that focus on geometric shapes or patterns tend to garner little interest. This does not mean that if you enjoy creating geometric abstract paintings, you will never be able to be successful as an artist. It simply means that, if you want to turn your art into a business, these are not the types of artworks you want to focus on when building your online presence.

Another good way to determine what types of artworks will sell well online is to take advantage of art-related discussion boards. Through your virtual conversations with other artists, you will get a sense of what types of art people have used to build successful online businesses.

A third method for identifying popular styles and genres of art online is to use a keyword tool such as **www.wordtracker.com** or the Overture keyword search tool available at **http://inventory. overture.com** to find out how many searches are done each month for particular types of art. For example, if you find there were 1,000 searches conducted for "landscape art" but only 50 for "abstract art," you will know that landscape art probably generates more online sales than abstract art. You can use this information to decide which types of art you should offer on your Web site and on online auctions.

13

Selling Your Handmade Crafts Online: Marketing Your Unique Creations

You may not think of the Internet as a place where you can sell handmade crafts. Most people who think of selling their crafts envision craft malls, flea markets, and other local events that can have you sitting in a lawn chair answering questions for passers-by all weekend.

Although local events are traditionally the venues people use to sell handmade crafts, the Internet has significantly increased the demand and availability of these items. Handmade toys, decorations, quilts, clay figurines, dolls, and mosaics can all be successfully sold on the Internet. No matter what types of crafts you make, a comprehensive marketing plan can help you earn a substantial income offering these products online.

There are several ways you can sell your crafts on the Internet:

Selling Through Your Web Site

The first way of making money with your handmade crafts online is selling to individuals by using a traditional Internet marketing approach. You can use many of the same tools and techniques that fine artists use to sell their artworks — a dedicated business Web site, auction listings, blogs, informational articles, discussion board postings, e-mail courses, and newsletters. All these will help you put your handmade crafts in front of visitors who will be happy to purchase these items for their homes.

When building your Web site, make sure visitors can easily find the types of crafts they are looking for. It is less important that you create a sense of continuity with a crafting Web site than with a fine art Web site, but you will still want to group your different types of crafts together on separate pages so visitors do not have to spend hours wading through the offerings on your site to find what they are looking for.

For example, if you sell several different types of crafts, you may create separate pages for groups of items such as glasswork, porcelain dolls, wicker baskets, hanging quilts, and decorative vases. The easier you make it for your visitors to find what they want, the more likely you will be to sell enough items to make a living with your online crafting business.

Selling Through Cooperative Web Sites

You can also market your crafts through cooperative Web sites, which offer items from many different crafters. These Web sites handle all the search engine marketing and draw hundreds of visitors each day who are looking for unique crafts for their homes.

There are many cooperative crafting Web sites available for promoting and selling your handmade crafts. One of the largest cooperatives is **www.craftmall.com**. This Web site allows crafters to sell items in dozens of categories, including Americana, candle holders, decoupage, and leather crafts.

Craftmall also features a shopping cart function, so people can purchase crafts directly from the site and pay for them with a credit card.

Another excellent Web site for selling your crafts is **www. handmadecatalog.com**. This Web site offers similar features as Craftmall but also allows you to purchase a Professional Membership, which places your name on the site's front page. This draws even more traffic to your craft listings, which can help you substantially increase your sales.

Handmade items can also be promoted and sold on **www.etsy. com**. This can be an economical way to promote your handmade crafts, because it costs only $0.20 per item to list crafts on this Web site. Many crafters, and quite a few people whose work blurs the line between fine art and craft, have experienced success with listing items on this Web site.

Selling Through Online Auctions

Another way to sell your crafts is to place items for sale on auction sites such as eBay. Selling crafts on eBay can be a bit greater of a challenge than selling fine art, because there is currently no dedicated category for handmade crafts.

Some crafters list their items in the "Self-Representing Artists" category with mixed success. People who browse this category may be looking for paintings for their homes or offices or, to a lesser extent, fine art sculptures. These people may pass over your auctions not because your items are undesirable, but because they had another type of item in mind.

You may want to look for categories that more closely match the types of crafts you are selling, such as Collectibles, Toys, or Jewelry. In your listing text, you can emphasize that your items are handmade and that because of this fact, people can purchase your items and know that their neighbors will not have identical items. People like to feel special and unique, and by highlighting the unique nature of your crafts, you can tap into this need to entice your auction viewers to bid on and purchase your crafts.

Selling Your Music Online: Bringing Your Music to the Masses

The demand for music on the Internet is greater today than ever. With the advent of portable media devices such as the Apple iPod, Internet users can easily download digital music and take it with them wherever they go, without the need for cumbersome CDs.

Not only that, but people use the Internet to find new, interesting music they cannot find through the large music stores such as Virgin Records. Many Internet users delight in finding independent music artists that are not afraid to experiment with elements of music and create new subgenres to express their creative visions.

This gives you the opportunity to market your music in an environment where uniqueness is appreciated and where you do not have to conform to the formulas of major music labels to be successful.

Marketing your music on the Internet also gives you the opportunity to attract independent and major music label representatives, who can help you reach more customers both online and offline.

Many of the marketing elements that apply to visual artists will also work well for musicians. Like any creative artist, you should have a dedicated Web site and a blog to promote your recorded music and live shows. As previously noted, you can also use Web sites such as MySpace to raise the visibility of your work and give users the chance to hear your music for themselves.

Advantages of Selling Downloadable Music

Many music artists who want to promote their works think they need to record their music on cases of CDs and rely on a music label representative to distribute and promote their work. However, converting your recorded music to a downloadable format and promoting it on the Internet gives you a number of distinct advantages:

- ♪ **Low distribution costs.** It can cost thousands of dollars to record your music to CDs and have them distributed across the country or internationally. With downloadable digital music, you do not have to incur the expense of purchasing CDs, printing custom inserts, and recording your music to the CDs for distribution.

- ♪ **Reaching a global audience.** The success of all types of creative works depends on the particular tastes of people living in a certain country or region, but tastes in music vary even more around the world. Promoting downloadable music on the Internet gives you the opportunity to reach people all over the world and have a better chance of finding an audience that appreciates your musical works. For example, if you have assembled a cello rock quartet and have recorded several songs, you may find limited success in North America — this genre is considered to have a "cult following" rather than a large audience. In contrast, cello rock is considered more mainstream in certain parts of Western Europe, and so you are more likely to find a viable customer base in that region.

♪ **No shipping hassles.** People who like your music will pay for a song or album and download it immediately. You will not have to worry about packaging your CDs, taking them to the post office or other shipping service, and hoping that they reach their destinations without sustaining damage.

Here are some additional ways you can promote your music to build a successful online business:

iTunes

If you are signed to an independent or major record label or if you own an independent label in addition to being a musician, you can promote your work on iTunes. This Web site is owned by Apple and offers one of the easiest user interfaces available for purchasing and downloading songs and albums to iPods.

An iPod is one of the most popular brands of portable music players available today. The first iPods allowed owners to download only music files from the Internet and could store between 200 and 500 songs. Today, iPods not only allow owners to download music, but also videos, movies, and other types of media. The newest iPod versions such as the iPod Touch and the iPhone can also download media directly from the Internet via a Wi-Fi connection without the need for connecting to a PC or laptop, making it easier than ever for owners to download music and video on the go. These devices have become an indispensable part of many people's lives.

By making your music available through iTunes, you will be able to reach every person who owns an iPod — this gives you an audience of millions of music lovers around the world.

To get started selling your music on iTunes, you will need to fill out an application containing some basic information about you, your band, and your music label. The application is available at this case-sensitive Web site address:

https://phobos.apple.com/WebObjects/MZLabel.woa/wa/ apply

At any one time, iTunes is reviewing hundreds of applications, so it may take a few weeks before you receive a response. Having your digital music accepted on iTunes is not an easy or quick process, but the opportunity to promote your work and reach a large Internet audience is worth the time and effort it will take to have your work accepted and promoted by iTunes.

IndieTunes

Another excellent venue for promoting your downloadable music is IndieTunes. This Web site can be especially useful if you are signed to an independent music label or if you have not yet been signed to a label.

You can sign up for IndieTunes at **www.indietunes.com**. Instead of charging you every time your songs are downloaded from the Web site, IndieTunes offers a professional subscription package for $9.95 per month. This package allows you to promote your work whether you have one recorded song or an entire album to offer to customers. If you have album art of liner notes available, you can also make these available when users download your music to their iPods or other portable media devices.

Because IndieTunes does not charge you for customer downloads, you can use this to your advantage by allowing customers to download one or two tracks for free. This gives customers the opportunity to sample your music without risk and also lets them share your music with friends, which will help further promote your music without any extra effort on your part.

CDBaby

Another excellent resource for selling your music online is CDBaby. This website features music by independent musicians, and can help you market your music on iTunes, Napster, eMusic, and other music related Web sites. CDBaby also states that it will make your music available to 2,400 retailers in the United States.

You can sign up to sell your music at **www.cdbaby.net**. CDBaby charges a $35 setup fee to obtain an account and upload your music.

CDBaby also charges a per-purchase fee to musicians for each customer purchase. Currently, the Web site charges $4 per physical CD purchased, and 9% of the purchase price for digital downloads.

One advantage of CDBaby is that the Web site states it pays musicians weekly, rather than making musicians wait months to receive revenues from sales of their recordings.

EMusic

If you are signed to an independent label, you can also market your music on **www.emusic.com**. This Web site promotes a wide range of independent music from many genres and sub-genres, as well as eBooks.

There is very little information on the Web site about how artists are paid. The marketing portion of the site is tailored to owners and managers of independent labels, rather than to individual musicians.

It is important to note that even though eMusic can be an excellent tool for promoting your music, the Web site does not promote unsigned artists. If you have not been signed to an independent label, you will not be able to promote your music here.

Selling Your Photographs Online: Meeting the Demand for Unique Images

If photography is your passion, then this section of the book is for you. In this chapter, you will learn about ways to choose and photograph images that will sell. You will also learn about setting up an online gallery and getting in front of an audience that will be interested in buying your photographs.

Shooting What Sells: Choosing Images that People Will Buy

The key element to selling your photographs is finding and photographing images that people will want to buy while still being able to add your unique style and flair. As with any form of art, different things appeal to different people, so you have room to use your own unique style when creating and selling your photographs. The trick is getting them in front of the people they will appeal to.

There are some things to keep in mind when you are shooting photos that will appeal to your online audience. Your subjects need to evoke feelings and emotions in viewers — a person will be much more likely to purchase an image if he or she feels an emotional connection to the subject matter or the composition of the image. Your subjects must be famous, beautiful, interesting, haunting, thought-provoking, or making a strong political or environmental statement to sell well. Although photographs that do not possess these qualities may have buyers out there, they will not produce as much income as those that have these special traits.

You may also want to pick a category and do a series of images based on that category. Categories of photographic works create a sense of continuity in your portfolio. People tend to choose images by photographers that specialize in capturing images of certain subjects or with certain compositional traits. They tend to shy away from photographers that take images with a shotgun approach, capturing images of anything they think will sell online.

Creating a series of photographs within a category also gives your viewers many images with similar qualities to choose from. For example, if you are photographing a series of wine glass images, some people may want dark or light backgrounds; some may want a clean, simple composition or a busy, richly textured one; and some may prefer the wine glass itself to be on the left or right side of the image. This helps you deal with one of the unique challenges that selling creative works on the Internet poses — there are millions of images on hundreds of Web sites that Internet users can choose from, so if there is anything about an image that is not quite right, they will keep looking. Providing a large number of photographs in a series helps ensure that even if they keep looking, they are still looking at your works instead of someone else's.

Here are some examples of categories you can use to create a series of photographs. In many cases, you will want to explore a subcategory and create a series based on that subcategory, because many categories are too broad to create a sense of continuity when viewers browse your portfolio:

- **Abstract.** Many people who are browsing for photographic images online are looking for an abstract design to use as a Web site background or to integrate into an advertisement, newsletter, or other document. There is a nearly endless number of subcategories you can focus on when creating a series of abstract photographs — you can create a series based on a particular color scheme, a certain texture, the presence of certain shapes, or other images.

- **Animals.** You may want to create a series based on images of domesticated animals, such as cats, dogs, or saltwater fish, or on images of wild animals, such as deer, buffalo, lions, or tigers. Most often, a series of works should concentrate on one certain type of animal and may even concentrate on images of that animal in a specific setting, such as kittens playing in a wicker laundry basket. Images of animals can be used in numerous settings, from Web site design to fine art for a client's home, so they can be ideal for reaching a wide variety of buyers.

🎥 **Beauty** is a category that can be taken in a number of different directions. You could take a series of images focusing on the physical beauty of the female form, portraits of exceptionally good-looking men or women, the beauty of nature, or the even women touching up their makeup before they get out of the car. These images tend to be rather dramatic, with more of the polished, slick feel of an advertisement than is needed for other categories of photographs.

🎥 **Bridges** are a photographic subject that appeals to many people. You do not have to limit yourself to taking photographs of covered bridges in quaint rural settings (although these images often do sell well). You can also take photographs of modern bridges — close-ups of a bridge's structure can focus on the geometric patterns of a bridge's supports and the texture of the steel on bridges that have been exposed to the elements for years. Bridges and bridge underpasses are also common places for graffiti, so you could also create a series of urban portraits to capture graffiti art.

🎥 **Churches and Religious Sites.** The stained-glass windows and indirect lighting of many older churches provide an opportunity for images that are ethereal, haunting, or inspiring. You can easily evoke emotions with these types of images — think of a series of photographs of a lone figure sitting in a dimly lit chapel, bowing his or her head while candles burn at the altar. You can use churches and religious sites to create dramatic works that will strike a chord with many of your viewers.

- **Cities.** You may create a series of images focusing on a particular city, a certain type of city, or a certain section of a city, such as an old forgotten downtown section or a vibrant new suburban shopping area. Cities give you a wide variety of subtopics to choose from — architecture, businesses, and residential areas all provide limitless inspiration for images that are powerful and thought-provoking.

- **Desert Landscapes.** The solitude associated with the desert can create stark emotions in your viewers, so this can be a good category for a series of photographic works. Some photographers prefer to capture the vibrant pastel colors of a sunset splashing across the sand; others prefer take pictures of the desert in the early afternoon when the harsh sunlight creates a sense of desolation. Still others prefer to focus on the vegetation of the desert, capturing images of sparse cacti scattered across the horizon.

- **Diversity** is a good category if you would like to sell your images to businesses. Corporations, small businesses, and nonprofits all need images that convey a since of diversity for Web sites, training materials, sales brochures, and many other types of materials. When planning a series of images in this category, take a few minutes to think about what diversity means to you — you can use the images that pop into your mind as the basis for your photographic compositions.

- **Flowers** give you wide latitude to create an image series that will be appealing to a wide audience. You can concentrate on a certain petal color, a specific type of flower, or a certain setting — a series of images depicting red roses in a crystal vase will appeal to a different group of viewers than red roses growing on a rose bush along a wooden fence. Flower images can also be used in everything from advertisements to fine art, so you can market these images in several formats and to several types of buyers.

- **Graveyards** make excellent places to create texture studies, capture a bit of history that is crumbling away, or simply create a group of images that will appeal to ghost chasers.

- **Growth.** Like diversity, growth can be explored in a number of different ways. You could capture the concept of growth by taking images of bean sprouts poking out of the soil in the late spring, or you could capture it by taking images that represent personal growth such as a woman being handed a college diploma at a graduation ceremony. The possibilities of this category are nearly limitless — you can easily find a unique way to express positive growth through your photographs just by thinking about what growth looks like to you.

- **Happiness.** You could create a photographic series based on children playing at the park, couples holding hands while strolling down the sidewalk, or the expression on a grandmother's face as she holds her grandson for the first time. Use your creativity to find unique ways to express happiness — it is a good way to build a photographic series that your viewers will emotionally connect with.

- **Historical Landmarks.** There are so many historical landmarks all over the world that photographers could probably never take enough pictures to cover them all. Do not just think of the major historical landmarks, such as Stonehenge and the St. Louis Arch, but also local landmarks, such as your community's first library or the original mayor's house.

- **Holiday.** You can capture and sell photographic images based on any holiday. You do not have to limit yourself to the major ones — you could create a whimsical series of photographs on Groundhog Day, Boss's Day, or National Author's Day.

- **Humorous.** Kittens playing with dogs and children acting silly are classic subjects for humorous photographs, but you can use your imagination to come up with other ideas for a series of humorous images. If you pick the right subject matter, you may end up with a series that sells well — people like to buy things that make them laugh.

- **Industry.** This is another category that can be lucrative, because you can attract the attention of businesses that need these images for various promotional materials, both online and offline. You can provide stock photos depicting activities associated with certain industries, but you may also seek contracts for this type of work so you can provide images depicting the specific facet of the industry desired by the buyer.

Love. You can create photographs depicting the concept of love in many ways. A series of images of a couple enjoying a candlelight dinner, a mother embracing her daughter, or a family wandering through the woods can all be good ideas for evoking emotions from your viewers. Images depicting scenes of love make good fine art for hanging in a home and can also be good images for family and relationship-oriented Web sites.

Luxury. A spacious hotel room, a Mercedes Benz parked on a brick paved driveway, a woman lounging beside a sparkling pool, and a pile of $100 bills on an oak desk can all be used to create images that convey a sense of luxury. Use your creativity to come up with scenes that make your viewers dream of incredible wealth, pampering, and happiness, and you will instill feelings in your viewers that will make them want to purchase your images to use on Web sites and in promotional print materials.

Mountains. Many people are fascinated with the majesty of mountain scenes. You can concentrate solely on the colors and shapes of a mountain range, or you can use mountains to convey other concepts, such as achievement, excellence, or spiritual growth. Although this is a common category, it is easy to use images of mountains in new and creative ways to create an original series of photographic images.

- **Nature.** Because many of us spend our days indoors, staring at the off-white walls of windowless offices while we work, we gravitate toward images of nature. Photographs of rolling hills, towering trees, and rushing streams give people a break from their day-to-day working lives. You can create a profitable portfolio by choosing an aspect of nature that interests you and creating a series of images based on your choice.

- **Oceans.** Water is associated with calmness, serenity, and whimsical adventure. Ocean scenes make people dream of carefree days and romantic nights. You can use images of oceans to evoke these feelings in your viewers — like nature scenes, oceanic images can be a welcome departure from the workaday world that your clients will appreciate.

- **Peace.** There are many ways you can use the concept of peace to create a series of images. You can address this subject from a political standpoint or focus on scenes that convey a sense of inner peace. A little brainstorming will yield numerous ideas for using this concept to create unique and compelling photo compositions.

- **People.** This is another extremely broad category but one you can use to sell quite a few images. Images of human beings are favorites among buyers of photographic images, because we naturally connect with images of people and because human subjects can be used to convey every emotion imaginable. You may want to create a series based on a particular human emotion or concentrate on a specific type of person — the young beautiful woman, the hard-working fireman, and the learned college student are a few examples of how humans can be used to create engaging photographs.

- **Places.** You can use this category to think of endless possibilities for your photographs. You could create an image series based on small towns, large cities, county villages, national parks, and other places.

- **Power.** There are many ways you can use a photographic series to convey a sense of power. Tall buildings, rushing waterfalls, earth-moving equipment, and lightening storms are a few examples of how you can express power through your photographs.

- **Rural Culture.** Many people, even those who live in urban areas, enjoy images of rural life. An Amish barn-raising or a farmer harvesting grain can make an excellent series of photographs. Also, visit village festivals or take a stroll down a country lane to get more ideas for images.

- **Schools.** Old one-room schoolhouses, elementary schools, high schools, and colleges provide excellent opportunities for you to create images for sale.

- **Spirituality.** A cross standing outside a country church, a weathered Buddha statue sitting at a temple entrance, and a lotus flower drifting along the surface of a pond can all convey a sense of spirituality. Because this concept means so many different things to people, you can approach this category in a number of ways to create powerful, emotional photographs.

- **Trees.** Images of trees can convey many emotions and concepts because of the settings where they are located and because of the way trees change appearance throughout the year. A cluster of forest redwood trees can convey a sense of strength and power, while white blossoms blooming on cherry trees can evoke feelings of hope and renewal.

This list is merely an example of different types of categories for your pictures. This is your artistic vision; therefore, the possibilities are endless as long as you are able to breathe life into your work and take compelling pictures.

Another element to producing work that will sell is knowing the trends and the market. Trends in photography can sometimes emerge quickly, and other times trends will change slowly. Keeping updated on what is in demand is essential in creating work that will sell.

One way to get a sense of what types of images are currently selling is to visit one of the many stock photo Web sites on the Internet, such as **www.istockphoto.com, www.bigstockphoto.**

com, and many others. You can browse image categories to see how many times each image on the site has been purchased. With a little research, you will begin to notice the subjects and compositions that are attracting the most attention.

Selling Your Photographs on Your Web site

Just like artists who sell fine art paintings and sculptures online, when building your online photography gallery, you should strive to build a sense of continuity throughout your image galleries. Continuity makes it much easier for viewers to identify your photos as uniquely yours and helps create a brand for your business. You do not have to limit yourself to shooting the same subject over and over again, but you should either create continuity by grouping your images in the same category or grouping photos by purpose.

Grouping by Category

When using this technique, your galleries should contain only photos that relate to the same category and perhaps even the same subcategory. You may have several galleries on your Web site that reflect different subcategories within the same category.

For example, you may have several galleries that fall under the category of flowers. Each gallery within that collection may concentrate on different subcategories of flowers, such as roses, water lilies or cut flowers. You may create several galleries with images of roses of different colors — red, white, yellow, fire and ice, or pink. Over time, you will attract visitors who will be able to instantly identify images as your photographs.

Grouping by Purpose

Another way to quickly build a loyal client base is to group your photographs by purpose. Some buyers look for images to add to Web site designs, blogs, and other online marketing materials. Other buyers look for images to use for books and magazines. Still others seek images to display as fine art in homes, offices, and corporate board rooms.

Grouping your images according to purpose will help you to attract clients who know you will have a variety of images available to meet their business and personal needs. They will come back to you time and time again, viewing you as a reliable resource for compelling, well-composed images. Some clients will even ask you to create special images just for them, and you will be able to command higher prices for these commissioned assignments because your clients know your work and trust you to successfully carry out their wishes.

This method of creating continuity in your image galleries will also allow you to receive referrals from clients and easily convert these referrals into paying customers, because they will quickly be able to see that you understand their needs. Over time, this technique can help you build a client base that will provide the bulk of your income, which means you can spend less time working to attract buyers and more time doing what you love — taking pictures that people are eager to buy.

Selling Your Photographs on Stock Photo Sites

In addition to marketing your photographs on your Web site and blog and promoting your images with online auctions, articles, e-mail broadcasts, and other marketing tools, you can also sell your images on stock photo Web sites.

A stock photo Web site is a place where individual photographers can place their images for sale and people looking for images to use on Web sites and in print materials and other media can browse all the images provided by photographers.

As a photographer, signing up for a stock photo Web site gives you several advantages:

- 📷 It allows you to market you images on sites that receive thousands of paying visitors each day. By uploading your photographs on a stock photo Web site, you will be tapping into a successful marketing vehicle without having to handle any of the promotion of the site yourself. You will have a team of marketers working for you, building your success while they grow the site you have placed your photographic works on.

- 📷 It gives you the opportunity to sell the same image over and over again, with no additional work. Compelling images can attract hundreds of buyers who are willing to pay to download your images, and you will receive a portion of the profits from each download.

- It allows you to quickly build a reputation as a professional photographer and build a loyal client base that will buy your images again and again. Visitors can search for images using your name, so they can quickly see all the images you have available on a particular stock photo Web site. They may purchase several images within a particular series or browse and buy from any of the other collections you offer.

- You will not have to worry about packaging and shipping your photographs. Because images on stock photo Web sites are available to buyers only in digital format, people can purchase your works and download them immediately — no buying mailers to protect your photos, no trips to the post office, no guessing how much postage is required to get your images to your customers.

Of course, there are some disadvantages to selling your images on stock photo Web sites as well:

- Your images can be sold to individual customers for just a few dollars. You can use stock photo Web sites to build a good supplemental income if you have a variety of photos available, but relying on these sites to afford a good living can be a difficult proposition when customers are able to download your images for just a dollar or two each.

- You will have to share all purchases with the stock photo Web site. After fees have been deducted, you may earn only $0.50 for some purchases, making it even more difficult to earn a substantial income from the sale of your images.

Although selling photos on stock photo Web sites is a difficult way to earn a living, it can be an excellent way to earn extra income while building your reputation and establishing a strong presence online.

Payment, Packaging, & Shipping Considerations

After you have sold a creative work online, you will need to take care of the tasks of receiving payment from your customer and packaging and shipping your creative work. This chapter will briefly outline some of the considerations for taking care of these tasks while taking minimal time away from creating and promoting your other creative works.

Payment for Your Items

Before your customers purchase your works, you should let them know what payment methods are available. If you do not make this clear before a customer commits to a purchase, you may have a difficult time receiving payment from the client.

Many Internet users assume if they are purchasing something online that they will be able to make payment with a credit card on the Web site they purchased the item from. If you do not accept credit cards on your Web site, make this clear on your Web site or auction listing.

Here are the most common payment methods you can make available to your customers:

Credit Card Payments Made Directly on Your Web site

This method is the most convenient for your customers — they can enter their credit card numbers on the ordering page, click the submit button, and complete their transaction in just a minute or two.

Offering this payment is a little more complicated for Web site owners. First, you have to purchase a merchant account with the ability to process online transactions. A merchant account is a special bank account used to accept credit card payments from consumers. When you apply for a merchant account, it will be underwritten just like any other type of financial account. The company offering the merchant account will evaluate your business, the amount of transactions it anticipates that you will generate, and the condition of your credit.

It can cost several hundred dollars to set up a merchant account and integrate it into your Web site. You also have to make sure the payment authorization interface used by the merchant account company is compatible with the shopping cart software used by your Web site's hosting company, if your hosting company offers a shopping cart feature.

Merchant account providers charge fees for each transaction that is processed in addition to any setup or maintenance fees. Transaction fees are between 2 and 4 percent of the total purchase price, depending on the provider and the type of merchant account you select.

Unless you are selling a large volume of works on your Web site, opening a merchant account can prove to be a costly and cumbersome payment solution.

PayPal

PayPal offers an alternative to purchasing and integrating a merchant account into your Web site. You can still accept payments by credit card, but when making payment, customers are redirected to a PayPal page to enter their payment information.

PayPal is substantially easier to use than a merchant account, because you do not have to worry about integrating anything or setting up a virtual shopping cart on your Web site. You can simply copy a snippet of HTML code available when you register for your free account at **www.paypal.com**, and paste it into your Web site to give your customers the ability to pay you through PayPal.

When payments are made through PayPal, the funds are deposited into an account available on your secure PayPal page. You can withdraw these funds to your own personal checking or savings account for free — it takes three or four business days for the funds to appear in your personal account.

You can also get a PayPal debit card, which will allow you to make purchases at any retailer that accepts credit cards and debit the funds from your PayPal balance. This can be a good way to keep your personal and business finances separate — you can use the PayPal money to pay for supplies, Web site hosting, shipping, and other costs related to your business, instead of using your personal checking account.

Like merchant accounts, PayPal charges a percentage of the total amount of each payment you receive, plus a nominal processing fee. Currently, 2.9 percent of each transaction, plus an additional $0.30 for processing, is deducted from each payment that is deposited into your PayPal account. If you happen to receive more than $100,000 in payments each month, PayPal will drop the transaction fee to 1.9 percent.

PayPal also allows you to accept funds via electronic checks. To you, there is virtually no difference between receiving a payment funded by a credit card and a payment funded by an electronic check, except that it may take a few days for an electronic check to clear, so you may not have immediate access to those funds.

Checks and Money Orders

If you want to attract the most customers possible, you can also offer to accept payment via a personal check or money order mailed to you. A few artists still do this, but most have had a bad experience or two with offering these payment methods and have decided to stick to electronic payments.

If you allow a customer to pay by personal check, you will not only have to wait for the check to arrive in the mail, but you will also have to wait for the check to clear. If it does not clear, then you are stuck trying to collect the returned check fee charged by your bank in addition to the purchase price of your artwork.

There are few people who will base their purchasing decisions on whether you accept mailed checks or money orders, so there is little advantage to leaving the door open for people to pay you by personal check. It is more hassle than it is worth for most artists — the time you spend trying to collect payment from customers who pay by check could be better spent creating artworks or promoting your Web site.

If you do decide to accept personal checks, it is important that you do not ship the artwork until the payment clears. No matter how nice the customer seems or how eager he or she is to hang your artwork in his or her living room, you have no assurance that the payment will clear. If you have already shipped the item before a customer's check is returned for insufficient funds, you are going to have a difficult time collecting valid payment from that customer.

Packaging Your Creative Works

Once you have received payment for an artwork, handmade craft item, photograph, or music CD, you will need to consider how to package your item for shipping. You will not want your customers to receive items that are broken, damaged, or in a condition other than what you promised. If a customer receives a damaged work, you will be expected to compensate the customer.

Making a customer happy when he or she receives an original artwork that is damaged is more difficult than if you were selling a mass-manufactured consumer product such as a toaster or an iPod, because the item can never be truly replaced. Your customer paid for a unique item, so you cannot just send him or her another item to make up for the inconvenience. Many times, the best you can do is to refund the purchase price and any packaging and shipping costs paid by the customer and perhaps pay for the shipping costs your customer incurs in sending the damaged item back to you.

Because it is important that your customers receive your creative works in perfect condition, it is a good idea to take every precaution to make sure the item is properly packaged before it leaves your studio.

You essentially have two options when packaging your item. If you do not have time to package your artworks yourself, you can use a service such as the UPS Store to package your items for you. You can find UPS Store locations at **www.ups.com.** The employees at your local UPS Store will select the correct packaging for your item and carefully pack it to minimize the risk of damage. You can also insure the item against damage so that if an artwork does arrive in poor condition, UPS will pay the cost of refunding your customer's payment for the artwork and shipping costs.

Using a service to package your items for you can be expensive, and you will have to ship the item through that service as well. For large artworks, it is not unusual to incur costs of $100 or more when you use a service to package and ship an item.

Unless you are shipping artworks with a purchase price of $1,000 or more, it is not cost-effective to use this type of service to provide your packaging needs.

The other option is to package the items yourself or hire someone to package them for you on a per-item basis. This will save quite a bit of money on your packaging costs, and you can pass these savings along to your customers.

You can purchase packaging supplies at your local shipper or order them from major shipping companies, such as **www. usps.com, www.ups.com, www.fedex.com,** or **www.dhl.com.** Ordering your packaging supplies online will save you the time you would otherwise spend driving to your local shipping store to pick up supplies.

You can save more money by buying your shipping supplies at **www.uline.com**. Uline carries a wide variety of cardboard boxes in many different sizes, as well as bubble wrap, plastic wrap, packaging tape, and any other supplies you may need to make sure that your creative works are securely packaged. When purchasing boxes from Uline, you will have to buy them in bulk — for example, if you are buying flat boxes to ship paintings, you may need to buy them in units of 10 or 25. Doing this can save you time, though, because you will have all the supplies you need to package and ship several artworks, instead of running to the store to get packaging supplies every time a customer makes a purchase.

Packaging your creative works yourself also gives you the peace of mind that comes with knowing your items are packaged correctly. You will not have to worry about whether a packaging service has selected materials that will adequately ensure your item will arrive free from damage.

Whether you choose to use a packaging service or package your creative works yourself, you will be able to pass the costs of packaging along to your customer. It is a good idea to determine how much you will spend for packaging supplies before you place your item for sale, so you can let your customers know up front how much they will pay for packaging. You may also want to explain how you will package your works and stress the importance of proper packaging so that your customers will understand why they are expected to pay a substantial amount for packaging costs. When your customers understand you are committed to packaging items so they arrive damage free, they will have no problem with paying whatever you ask for packaging materials.

Shipping Your Works

After you have packaged an item you have sold online, you will need to arrange shipment of the item. There are a few things you should consider when choosing how to ship your item:

- **The shipping costs.** Although you will be able to pass your shipping costs on to your customers, you will want to keep these costs as low as possible, especially if you are offering your creative works at a discount. Your customers will not want to pay more in shipping costs than for the artwork itself, so it may not be feasible to use a shipping service to package and ship your artworks. The lower the shipping costs for an item, the more customers will be willing to pay for your works. If a client buys more than one work, you may also want to combine shipping for the items by packaging the works in the same box whenever possible to further reduce your customer's costs.

- **The shipping time.** Customers who purchase your works through your Web site or eBay auctions will be excited about receiving their artworks. Deciding how you will package and ship a particular item before you place it online for sale will help you reduce the time between when the customer purchases your item and when he or she receives it.

- **Where your customer is located.** Large packages may be difficult to ship internationally and may take two weeks or more to reach your customers. If an international client purchases one of your works, you may want to let him or her know up front that it may take a while for the package to arrive. If your client is used to purchasing items internationally, he or she will understand and will not be deterred from completing a purchase.

- **The weight and size of the package.** Commercial shipping services such as UPS, DHL, FedEx, and USPS have restrictions on the weight and size of packages that can be shipped. For example, packages shipped via UPS must be less than 150 pounds and must have a combined length and girth of less than 165 inches.

To determine whether your package meets this size requirement, you must determine the length and girth of your package. The length is the measurement in inches of the longest side of your package. The girth is the total measurement of the height and width of your package times two.

For example, suppose you are shipping a package that is 60 inches by 40 inches by 6 inches. The length of your package is 60 inches, and the girth is (40 inches plus 6 inches) times two. The total measurement of the package is 152 inches, which is under the maximum shipping size allowed by UPS.

You may want to offer free shipping on artworks that sell for more than a certain amount during period when sales are slow. Keeping shipping costs low will allow you to offer this promotion more economically so you can still make a substantial profit.

Conclusion

Throughout the pages of this book, you have learned how to build an online business from the ground up to promote and sell your artworks. Even if you had never used the Internet before when you picked up this book, by now you should have the resources you need to build a profitable and rewarding business. Like any business, selling art online is neither easy nor free of frustrations. However, if you follow the steps described in this book, you will have a much greater chance of success than most people who dream of making a living from their creative works.

Keep this book close at hand while you are building your art business — you will want to refer to it often for tips on how to display, market, sell, and distribute your creative works.

The remainder of this book is divided into two appendices:

Appendix A contains a number of resources you can use while you are establishing your online presence. You will find things such as shipping services, Web site hosting companies, art supply retailers and wholesalers, and merchant account providers. This appendix can be a valuable resource when you are looking for tools and services to help you start and expand your business.

Appendix B contains numerous cases studies, which you can use to learn how real people have been able to sell creative works online. You will read accounts from seasoned veterans who have built strong online presences as well as beginning entrepreneurs who are just starting to make their mark in the online world.

Finally, there is a glossary of terms used throughout this book. Use it as a quick reference while you are building your online business.

Appendix A: Resources

Art Supplies

- www.cheapjoes.com

- www.dickblick.com

- www.misterart.com

- www.utrecht.com

Blogging Sites

- www.blogger.com

- www.livejournal.com

- www.wordpress.com

- www.xanga.com

Freelancers

- www.elance.com

- www.getafreelancer.com

- www.gofreelance.com

- www.guru.com

- www.mediabistro.com

- www.sologig.com

Merchant Account Providers

- www.gotmerchant.com

- www.merchantexpress.com

Shipping Services

- www.dhl.com

- www.fedex.com

- www.usps.com

- www.ups.com

Web Site Hosting

- www.godaddy.com

- www.ixwebhosting.com

- www.hostmonster.com

Appendix B: Case Studies

In this appendix, you will read about creative people who have already created successful online businesses and artists who, like you, are just beginning their foray into the world of online sales.

The insights offered by these entrepreneurs will show you that you can build a profitable online business selling your creative works online. You will find out what has worked for successful artists and learn from the mistakes they have made while working to establish an online presence.

As you read through these case studies, you may want to take notes so you can remember ideas for building your own business as well as mistakes to avoid so you can use your time and money efficiently.

You will also want to visit the Web sites of each of these entrepreneurs so you can see firsthand the results of their efforts.

CASE STUDY: JULIE LANDMAN

Julie Landman

Owner, Absolute Stock Photo

(508) 397-2955

www.absolutestockphoto.com

I happened into selling stock photography online thanks to my mother, Verna Bice. She is an avid stock photographer and had started selling her photography online for a couple of years before I took notice and saw a great opportunity to help out photographers like her sell their images online. I have a strong business and IT background with a love for art so I decided to take the plunge into stock photography. I began my research and started to construct Absolute Stock Photo.

Today, online sales comprise 100 percent of Absolute Stock Photo's business. All of our sales originate from our online library — we have tried other avenues such as eBay but found little success there because of a low demand for digital images on eBay.

Getting the business going was probably a much quicker process than most people experience online. We were lucky enough to have photographers send Absolute some business before we were "findable" on Google and other search engines. I'd say it took about two months to index well enough on search engines to be found.

Overall, Absolute Stock Photo gets about 50 percent of its business from Google searches and about 75 percent from search engines in general, so search engine marketing is extremely important for my business.

CASE STUDY: JULIE LANDMAN

There are several things I love about selling creative works online. I enjoy looking at the originality and creativity of my photographers on such a regular basis. I love looking at the beauty each of them is able to find and capture. I enjoy the relationships I have created with my photographers. With over 150 photographers I do not know all of them personally, but I do get to enjoy communicating with at least a quarter of them on a fairly regular basis.

One drawback to selling online is that I do not like disappointing my photographers — I want all of them to get lots of sales, but it just does not happen. I have had many photographers leave me because they did not get any sales in x number of months. Losing a photographer is a bummer — they put so much energy into uploading just to throw it all away with a click, and I do not know if they have a good reason to pull their images off or if it is pride or ego.

CASE STUDY: DIANE DOBSON-BARTON

Diane Dobson-Barton

Owner, Artist How-To

(620) 473-2166

www.artist-how-to.com

I began listing art on eBay in about 1996. I then created a basic Web site that has grown over the years. Today, online sales are at least 80-90 percent of my total sales.

I use eBay, Etsy, blogs (WordPress, Blogger, Live Journal), and networking sites (MySpace, Facebook, Indiepublic) to promote my online art business. However, my Web site is also a crucial element of my marketing efforts — it is vital to all of my business transactions.

Here is one of the difficulties I have experienced with selling art online:

CASE STUDY: DIANE DOBSON-BARTON

Oftentimes, a problem arises when customers do not read an auction completely so they do not understand what they are buying. I find this happens less on my personal business site, although the auction listings contain the same or similar information. I assume this has to do with the customer base viewing the material. With sites such as eBay, you have a wider demographic viewing your artwork than those looking at Artist-How-To.

I enjoy selling online because I prefer to work alone. I never have enjoyed dealing with people when selling my work. Selling online allows me to do what I love to do and not be concerned when selling if my hair is combed or if I am wearing the "right clothes." My shyness is so strong that, if possible, I would never deal with people at all. But it is necessary in order to do the job.

There is very little I dislike about selling art online, but I do have a difficult time shutting off work at the end of the day. I find my "in-box" is always full. From marketing, developing ideas, organizing, or getting down to creating, there is always something that needs my attention.

If I had to start over again, I would be more open to asking and accepting help from others. I find that I want to do it all myself. I only recently hired someone to create a graphic I needed. For a while I had a studio assistant to handle jobs such as shipping, etc., but overall, I wish I was better at delegating.

If you are thinking of building a business selling creative works online, start out slow. Build a strong body of work before you concern yourself with having a site. Show only the very best work. Realize that doing art as a business is a juggling act, and remember it is a business. Keep good records of all expenses and income. If you are not sure what to keep track of, and you live in the U.S., get your hands on a Schedule C tax form as an example of where to begin. Seek out advice from the Small Business Administration at **www.sba.gov** and your state's Arts Commission.

Although many people look for the perfect way to promote their artworks, I do not think there is just one way or method. However, there

CASE STUDY: DIANE DOBSON-BARTON

are some that work substantially better than others. Join groups and network with those interested in possibly purchasing your work. Submit your site to search engines; trade links with other artists whose work you respect. Create a blog of interest to your customers to draw them to your site. Only later, after you have exhausted all free methods, should you even consider other methods.

CASE STUDY: NINA KLAUSEN

Nina Klausen

www.nina.klausen.com

Right now, my Web site accounts for about 70 percent of my art sales. I use Etsy to market my work and generate sales.

I also have a blog, but it is incorporated into my Web site rather than being a separate blog.

My Web site has been a crucial aspect of building my online business and generating art sales. I did not want to just set up a standard portfolio with some big faceless art-selling Web site where I am one of a million artists lumped into the same package and design. I wanted to custom-build the entire experience for my clients and have my work and my personality shine through in my Web site and every other aspect of my business.

One of the things I enjoy the most about selling art online is that I have customers from all over the world. I truly enjoy working to build and improve my Web site and the fact that I get to interact directly with my clients instead of dealing with them through a gallery representative.

One of the main drawbacks to selling art online is that customers do not get to physically see the artworks before purchasing them — there can be quite a few subtle differences between the way an artwork looks on a customer's computer monitor and the way it looks in real life.

CASE STUDY: NINA KLAUSEN

If I had to start my art business all over again, I would concentrate on fine art printmaking and put all of my other ventures aside. When I first started out, I was still freelancing as a graphic artist and illustrator, and I mixed this with my printmaking in one big, confusing mess of products and services.

If you are just starting out selling your creative works online, make sure that you have your own Web site, and make sure that it is professionally created and well designed. Your Web site should accurately reflect you and your work.

If you are not Web savvy and do not think that you will be able to keep your Web site updated, it is better to opt for a blog or a portfolio with one of the many online art sites. It is better to start small with something you can manage than to overextend yourself.

Also, always be polite and follow up on customer e-mails. Offer refunds when necessary. Internet shopping can be risky — most anything else purchased on the Internet can be returned, and art should be no exception.

CASE STUDY: KRISTEN QUEEN

Kristen Queen

kristenqueenart@yahoo.com

In my experience as a customer I find the ease, convenience, and audience of online sales is what encouraged me to further pursue the idea of moving my artwork online.

Though it will never replace physically going to a venue or gallery where artwork is showcased, it provides the overall convenience that many of us in today's hectic society can more easily work with based on our changing schedules.

CASE STUDY: KRISTEN QUEEN

Having only recently taken my artistic skills to a more professional level, I realized that in order to be profitable and reputable you need resources that can provide such opportunities. The Internet can readily provide multiple opportunities to both the emerging and seasoned artist, gathering from the multiple artists I have spoken with. It is conducive to my schedule and time.

Even with a change in the market demand, artwork is still alive and well on the Internet. Whereas local galleries were having a difficult task moving pieces out and bringing new works in, Internet sales from eBay to personal Web pages and professional galleries online were doing well.

Online sales provide more direct means of your net profit. Marketing your artwork from a personal Web site removes the hassle associated with "middlemen," concerning gallery brokers, agents, and other physical aspects of making your art accessible to the most inclined market, to include the hassle of transporting artwork, hanging artwork, all while according to someone else's schedule and commission fees.

While there are many art agents online that will charge you accordingly, I believe that a personal Web site and a successful marketing strategy is all one will need to be moderately successful in online sales. This is a very simple and realistic goal that is very appealing to someone like me.

In order to keep things more fresh and organized I am hoping to launch my Web site by the first of the year. I am looking at using SiteKreator as my Web hosting service. The Web site has a very attractive layout with online demos, archives of page samples, and free trials. Most Web hosting services do not provide this level of interest when attracting potential customers. SiteKreator, although unintentionally, has become synonymous with online art-based Web sites. They have done well to encourage that marketing niche. Being "artist friendly" is a plus for me.

This means that galleries, perspective clients, and other artists are now more accessible then ever to each other. Online sales is all about

CASE STUDY: KRISTEN QUEEN

networking; any additional intrinsic qualities pertaining to my specific market that a Web host can offer is something crucial to consider.

For my site I want to keep it simple, classy but interesting, and not too formal. The viewer should be concerned with the artwork. I look at it in this way: if I were driving past a building with an understated, boring, or poorly kept shop front, I would not stop. If it was too over the top and cheesy I would not stop. Even though either one may have exactly what I was looking for, but the first impression is what sells first! You have to sell the idea and the place before you sell the item inside.

I want my artwork showcased in an eye-catching way; however, I do not want all the bells and whistles that some sites have that then become overwhelming to the viewer. There are also a lot of people without high-speed connections. I need to be considerate and make my Web sites accessible and easy to navigate for those who both do and do not have high-speed connections. My navigation bar will contain a:

Home Page: With general information pertaining to my work.

Gallery Pages: To showcase my work. These may be subcategorized for equine, canine, wildlife, etc. My artwork will have a brief description to include Title, Medium, Surface, Price, and maybe a small personal note on the piece as well.

Work-In-Progress Page: To keep interest in my work. I will include artists.

Artist's Bio: With one to three pictures relating to my artwork and my personal interests. I am primarily an equine artist; therefore, I will most likely be with a horse in my photos or other animals. People like to see this; it shows closeness to the artist's subjects and a personal connection.

Beneath the bio I will have my credentials, shows I have entered, pieces I have won for, etc.

Price List page: These will be specific. I will also give brief synopsis of

CASE STUDY: KRISTEN QUEEN

my medium and specialized surface that I use as selling points. I will also have reference comments from clients.

Contact page: Providing my name, my studio name, a P.O. Box, business phone number, and e-mail. No personal info relating outside of the business.

My plan is to launch my Web site and follow my niche in the physical market as well, for example, equestrian artwork. Become a vendor and on weekends travel to horse shows and events, have prints available as well as on useful and decorative items. I will have originals for sale as well but focus on my prints. I will also have originals and hope these will help build commissions orders. I hope the majority of my business online will come from generating the interest and beginning of sales at these events but further that momentum by being accessible online. For as many events as I have gone to, I will visit with vendors and like what they have there, but they may have something else or can do a custom piece through an online order. I love seeing people's Web sites after seeing what they had on display. Physical presence is more or less the tip of the iceberg in the market to me. Again by eliminating the hassle of transport, display, space and time, the Internet offers so much more. You do not have a ten-by-ten (area) with a collapsible tent and display racks; you have GBs of space, your own environment, and no bad weather. You can put everything up that you have to offer, not your best or what you think will sell at that particular event. No fuel costs! You are on display in the most conducive environment possible, and some things sell better online then they do in the real world.

I personally believe that you still have to be present in the physical world and be the face for your work and Web site in order to encourage traffic to get to you.

I feel that I have to be the billboard and ambassador for my business. I will probably get a pair of magnetic signs with my business card image on it, have my Web address clearly viewable, and attract the attention that way as well as being a vendor. The best thing people can do is

CASE STUDY: KRISTEN QUEEN

make themselves look good, have the physical and visible presence. You have to generate interest on the basic level in the flesh to get folks to type in your Web site address. Advertisement is still the reining supreme force of encouraging sales in this world. You have to direct people to you, and therefore the personal element I feel cannot be excluded when looking to make the move to online sales. This is the strategy that I will be using to generate business for my artistic career.

CASE STUDY: ELISA CHONG

Elisa Chong

Owner, Sofia Anime

www.sofianime.com

My Web site is like my business card online. It helps advertise what I do. About 80 percent of my transactions are online sales. Aside from my Web site, I use auctions, blogs, and social networking sites to promote my business.

One of my favorite things about selling online is meeting so many new fans and collectors and being able to chat with them. Having my art be collected all over the world. It is also a good way to advertise your art to anyone who has an Internet connection and can view the art all over the world.

One of the drawbacks of selling online is that it takes a little extra time to scan in the images, organize inventory, and pack and ship the items. It takes some of my time away from creating art.

If I had the opportunity to go back and change the way I built my online business, I would have started sooner. It is very exciting being able to meet so many collectors from all over the world and get inspiration from them for new paintings they want to see and commission me to do.

CASE STUDY: ELISA CHONG

One of the most important things you can do when building an art business online is to be very courteous to your fans and customers. Communicate well with them; offer a great product and good customer service at the same time.

Some of my best marketing methods are auctions and social networking sites and fan groups, who help promote my art all over the Internet.

CASE STUDY: SARAH ELIZABETH CONDOIN

Sarah Elizabeth Condoin

Owner, The Emergence Project

www.theemergenceproject.com

I got started selling art online with my conception of The Emergence Project, which is an online art gallery that promotes the work of a select group of emerging, avant-garde artists. There were several artists I was in contact with that needed and deserved gallery representation. I had been thinking about developing a Web site for a few years, and it finally came together in August 2007. I had to do a lot of research to find a cost-efficient method of designing and running a Web site. I went with the company NetFirms for hosting and e-mail.

Right now all of my sales are composed of online transactions. But I am planning on opening a physical gallery location within the next few years. Even then, I plan on utilizing the Web for a substantial portion of my sales. I do a lot of advertising and marketing. I also write articles and press releases about the goals and concepts of The Emergence Project.

Most of my marketing and advertising is done offline — in postcard mailings, magazine advertisements, etc. It is important to build your client list and market directly to them. However, I do use Google Ads and advertise on some of the major art collectors Web sites.

CASE STUDY: SARAH ELIZABETH CONDOIN

It took about two months to get my first sale. Of course, it takes time to establish yourself in the art world. But it is important to get exposure to as many people as possible. That is why the Internet is such a great resource. Even if people do not buy your work at the moment, you never know if five years from now they see your work in a gallery and remember it from your online Web site, and this would give them more motivation to buy it because they will feel that you are established and professional.

What I like about selling art online is that you know that the artwork is being seen by many people. That exposure is very important to me. It is also convenient for both myself and the customer.

What I dislike is that I do not have as much of the physical interaction with the artwork and with the customers.

If you are just starting out promoting and selling your art online, do not just sit back and think that your Web site is going to generate sales. You have to be actively promoting your Web site and bringing traffic to it. Also, make sure that the design of your site is well thought out and aesthetically pleasing. Make it easy to navigate and well organized. Make sure that the background color is neutral to show off the work well. Do not make the lettering on your site too big or small or in a hard-to-read font. Sometimes the littlest thing can detract away from your artwork. Make the design minimalist and neutral.

CASE STUDY: TANYA BOND

Tanya Bond

www.tanyabond.com

http://stores.ebay.com/Tanyas-Irish-Art

www.tanyabond.etsy.com

I started as a buyer on eBay, and then I realized that I might try to sell my art and it worked slowly but surely. Right now about 80 percent of my sales are done online. I have sold from my Web site only two times

CASE STUDY: TANYA BOND

so far, so my online business is mostly concentrated on eBay and a bit on Etsy. I believe having a blog helps generate extra visibility.

One of the few difficulties I have experienced with selling art online is that sometimes people prefer large artwork or framed under glass, which can easily be damaged while posted.

To me, the best thing about selling art online is surprise — the sales normally come when you least expect them. Also there is no shop/gallery setup cost, no need to look after it — so what you gain is a lot of free time that can be spent on creating more art. Huge audiences can be reached when selling online, and it's quite flattering to know that your works are being kept in collections all over the world.

If I had to start over again, I would not underprice my work from the very start. And I also would not get frustrated over very little sales in comparison with some established online sellers.

My best advice for people new to selling creative works online is this — do not expect miracles; generally, it takes several months if not years to get established online.

CASE STUDY: SUE STEINER

Sue Steiner

www.suesteiner.com

www.amish-art.com

www.amulti-coloredlife.blogspot.com

www.kidronarts.blogspot.com

Right now, only about 10 to 15 percent of my sales occur online, but I expect as I refine my audience this will increase.

My first online sale did not happen for several months after I began promoting my art online, but I do believe having the Web site helped in face-to-face meetings. People could see my work, and I feel it made a good impression.

CASE STUDY: SUE STEINER

I tried eBay but really could not find a niche. It felt too overwhelming to me so I did not pursue it. I have had good luck with blogs. I use that for networking and building a clientele. I like to do "work in progress" posts, and since I live in a tourist area I talk about how my area is an inspiration to me. I think people enjoy that personal touch of hearing how I am inspired and to watch artwork take shape. I think it's good for me as an artist too, because I put myself out there by allowing people in on the creative process.

I sometimes worry about the clumsiness of e-mail communication. I do horse and pet portraits, and I like to get a feel for the person and the animal. I think that happens better either in person or over the phone. I am a good talker but not as good of a typist!

One of the challenges of promoting and selling online is that it can be slightly addictive. Since the Internet never sleeps, you have to draw lines on how much time and energy you put into it. It can feel like a bottomless pit as far as possibilities. I try to make goals for myself and just keep chipping away at what I want to do with my art. I know I cannot do everything and do it well so I try to keep my focus on what is best for me.

CASE STUDY: LYNNE TAETZSCH

Lynne Taetzsch

3 Snyder Heights

Ithaca, NY 14850

607-273-1364

ARTBYLT.COM

Lynne@ARTBYLT.COM

I have always enjoyed working with computers as a user, not a programmer, and when I saw artists beginning to put their art on Web

CASE STUDY: LYNNE TAETZSCH

sites back in 1998, I decided to make one for my art. I began using the Netscape composer tool, which came with that browser then, in order to put together a simple Web site with my paintings on it. At that time, I used to photograph my paintings with an SLR camera outdoors to make slides. Instead, I had color prints made and then scanned them with a flatbed scanner in order to get the digital images for the Web site.

Over the years I continued to revise my Web site and to upgrade to more complex software for building it. For a few years I used Hotdog, which taught me a lot about HTML code. Finally, a few years ago, I bought Dreamweaver and took a class in how to use it. I also use a digital camera now to photograph the paintings and a flatbed scanner for drawings. I still do all my own design, coding, upgrading, promotion, etc., for my Web site.

In 2000, I made my first sales from the Web site. Sales were very slow at first but have gradually increased over the years.

I make 90 percent of my sales online. The rest are through galleries, word-of-mouth, and the Greater Ithaca Art Trail open studio weekends.

I have an art blog called All About Art, and for the last six months I've been making a drawing and writing about it every day in the art blog. Writing regularly increases readership. I also have a few videos on YouTube. I do not do auctions or eBay, but I am listed in some online group art sites. I've sold a couple paintings that way and do get some traffic from them.

My Web site has been the ultimate tool in establishing my presence online. It takes a lot of work, but it is definitely worth it. Not only do I make direct sales from it, but I hear from gallery owners, art consultants, and interior designers. I also get e-mails from other artists all over the world and have made many artist friends that way.

It took a couple of years before I made my first sale, but I think today that would not be the case. Back then, people were not as comfortable buying anything over the Internet, no less fine art. There are still many people who will not buy a piece of art unless they see it in person, but

CASE STUDY: LYNNE TAETZSCH

there are enough who will, and that number keeps growing. The important thing is to offer a money-back guarantee and to have a secure method for placing an order.

Some customers want to know the exact shade of red or green in a painting before they will buy it. In this case, I offer to send a printed photo of the work, which has helped to finalize sales. Every once in a while I come upon a difficult client who wants a better price, a Saturday delivery, or something else that costs me time, money, and aggravation. I have learned a lot over the years from dealing with problem customers like these. I've lost some sales and money, but the lessons have been invaluable.

I enjoy being able to reach people all over the world and having them love and praise my art. A gallery audience is limited to the people who walk in, but the Internet offers the possibility of unlimited worldwide exposure.

I also enjoy "talking" to people through the words I put on my Web site as well as e-mail exchanges. It gives clients a chance to get to know me and my art without having to come to a gallery reception to meet me.

The Internet is great for networking, and I have met many artists this way. We all help and encourage each other, and I've learned so much from them.

Shipping the art is always a challenge. When I think I've got it all figured out, the shipping company changes its rules or pricing, or the company that packs my art makes a mistake. Recently DHL Express lost a 48-inch by 48-inch box of art on its way to a customer. Finding good shipping solutions is one of the biggest challenges.

A problem shipping art internationally is customs. Often clients have to pay duty on the art that makes the cost prohibitive for them. This is related to the shipping problem, because shipping overseas is much more expensive also.

Maintaining an online art business takes a lot of work, and that takes

CASE STUDY: LYNNE TAETZSCH

away from the time I have to make art. I enjoy most of the business-work side, but sometimes it can get crazy. When I travel, I have to keep my notebook computer with me so I can stay in touch with customers.

Knowing what I know now, I would have started nine years ago with the Web site I have today. I learned as I went along, and I'm still learning. My Internet business is an ever-evolving process. One thing that is important is to choose your domain name carefully. Most artists use their own names, which is fine. I did not because I have a last name that's very difficult to spell. But sometimes there is a descriptive term that would be perfect for the kind of art you do. Think about the keywords your customer may type into Google or Yahoo! search to find your kind of art. Maybe a descriptive title would be better to use than your name. Once you have a domain name, you never want to change it because you'll lose whatever momentum you've got started. So take your time and find a good one.

Make sure the images on your Web site are a positive reflection of the actual art. And do not forget textual content. Search engines look for text, and if you want people to see your art, you'd better think about how they will find it. Building the Web site is only the first step. Figuring out how to get people to look at it cannot be ignored. It's an art in itself.

Rich textual content will also help sell your art. Not everyone will read it, but many will. This is a chance to tell your visitors who you are, how you make your art, and what it means to you.

I try to use every tool available to help people find my Web site. I exchange links with other art Web sites, I have videos on YouTube, I have written articles for syndication with links back to my site, I write press releases and distribute them, and I have an art blog. All the pieces start to build an audience. I do not think I can single out any one of them as the most effective. There are always new ones coming along, like MySpace, Facebook, Second Life, and Squidoo. That's why there is never enough time to do everything possible in terms of online marketing.

Author Dedication & Biography

This book is dedicated to my patient and loving wife, Carla, who inspires me and encourages my creative side, and my daughter, Aria, who has taught me to embrace each day with joy and gratitude.

....

Lee Rowley is a professional writer and artist working in the Columbus, Ohio, area. He received his B.S. in Art from the University of Rio Grande in 1997 and is currently pursuing an M.B.A. He has been selling abstract and surrealist artworks online and offline for several years under his own name and under the guise of a tuxedoed, gas-mask-wearing hermit named Fall Out Bob.

When not writing or creating art, Lee enjoys traveling with his wife, Carla, and their daughter, Aria.

Affiliate link: A link contained on a Web site that directs a visitor to another Web site offering products or services for sale. A Web site owner who places an affiliate link on his or her site has previously entered into an agreement with the Web site offering the products or services, which allows the referring Web site owner to earn a portion of sales derived from the referral. Affiliate links contain a unique identifier that helps the product site owner track referrals and pay commissions to affiliates.

Affiliate program: A revenue-sharing program used by Internet marketers to increase sales or to gain income from referring buyers to another Web site offering products or services for sale. Web site owners who sell products or services on a Web site may offer affiliates a percentage of any sales derived from a referral provided by the affiliate.

Alt tag: A short block of text associated with an image placed on a Web site. Web site owners use alt tags to provide a short description of the image, and most include keywords in the description in an effort to boost a Web page's ranking in search engine listings for specific keywords.

Article directories: Web sites that accept, categorize, and publish article content written and submitted by individual authors. Web site owners write articles for publication and submission to article directories, and users can select articles from a directory for publication on their own Web sites. Article directories allow the authors to gain additional exposure for their Web pages.

Article marketing: A marketing strategy in which a Web site owner writes free, informative articles and submits them to article directories for publication. Although article authors do not derive income directly from these articles, the authors benefit by including their Web site addresses and biographical information in the resource boxes that appear at the end of each article.

Artist group: An online gathering place for artists, crafters, photographers, or other creative professionals. Artist groups use discussion boards, chat rooms, and other means for artists to share ideas, participate in contests, and collaborate on creative works. Artist groups also allow an artist to create a profile that can be used to promote creative works on other Web sites.

Auction listing: A specific page on eBay or other auction site that users can visit to learn about and place bids on an item you have posted for sale. Auction listings for creative works such as paintings, sculpture, handmade crafts, and photographs contain one or more images of the work, as well as a text description to describe the size of the work, the materials used in its construction, and other information to build interest and entice users to bid on the item.

Autoresponder: A software program or Web-based application that allows you to compose and send e-mails to e-mail marketing subscribers at specified intervals. E-mails can be sent to all your e-mail list subscribers at once or can be triggered by a Web site visitor's completion and submission of a CGI form. Autoresponders can save Internet marketers a substantial amount of time by managing promotional e-mails without constant monitoring.

Bandwidth: The total size of files that are transferred when each Web site visitor accesses a Web page or downloads files from a page. The larger the files on a Web site, the greater the bandwidth used to display those files on a visitor's Internet browser. Hosting providers place a monthly limit on the amount of bandwidth that can be generated by visitors accessing a Web site and charge the Web site owners overage fees when bandwidth is exceeded during a given month.

Blog: Short for Web log. In its most rudimentary form, a blog is a series of text entries similar to a diary. Entries can be displayed in chronological or reverse chronological order. Blogs are used by businesses to promote products or services as well as by personal users to keep family or friends up to date. People can integrate blogs into Web sites or create separate blogs that contain links and references to the Web sites.

Broadcast e-mail: An e-mail sent to all subscribers at one time. Broadcast e-mails may be used to send special information or to alert subscribers to special offers or discounts on products available on the sender's Web site.

Browser: An interface that allows Web site visitors to access and view Web pages on a personal computer. Different browsers can display Web pages differently, so when a Web site owner is creating pages for his or her site, it is important for the owner to ensure the pages will display correctly on commonly used browsers. Common browsers include Internet Explorer, Netscape, and Mozilla Firefox.

Business plan: A detailed document that describes a business, identifies its owners and key personnel, and outlines the plans the business owners have for future growth. This document is necessary for business owners who wish to attract potential investors or business loans from financial institutions. It is also a valuable document for people just starting a business, because it gives them a detailed blueprint to follow as the business grows and encounters new challenges.

Common Gateway Interface (CGI) form: A series of text boxes placed on a Web site to gather information about a Web site visitor. CGI forms can capture a visitor's name, e-mail address, artistic preferences, or any other information an artist wishes to use to decide how to promote his or her creative works. Information entered into a CGI form by a Web site visitor is processed and sent to the artist's e-mail inbox.

Dial-up: An Internet connection that uses a telephone line connected to a port on a computer. Dial-up connections produce significantly slower page loads than high-speed Internet connections and can make navigating, building, or editing a Web site a time-consuming process.

Discussion board: A section of a Web site where users may post thoughts, opinions, news, or other content about a particular subject. Other users may then respond to these messages, creating an asynchronous discussion that may go on for several pages. Discussion boards may contain hundreds or thousands of discussions.

Domain: The root address under which all pages of a Web site are grouped. A domain must be purchased or otherwise reserved by a Web site owner before a Web site can be published to the Internet. If an artist chooses the domain name www.joesmithartgallery.com, all pages of the Web site will use this domain as the root of its URL. Examples: www.joesmithartgallery.com/home, www.joesmithartgallery.com/paintings, www.joesmithartgallery.com/contact_me.

E-mail course: Instructional e-mail(s) designed to improve readers' knowledge about a topic related to the sender's Web site or business. E-mail courses may consist of a single e-mail transmission or may be broken into several parts sent at designated intervals to give the sender more opportunities to contact the subscriber and remind him or her of products or information available on the Web site.

E-mail marketing: An Internet marketing technique by which a Web site owner promotes his or her products via e-mails sent to newsletter subscribers. E-mails may also be sent that are purely informational to build subscriber trust and loyalty. A Web site visitor must voluntarily offer his or her e-mail address before the Web site owner can legally include the visitor in an e-mail marketing campaign.

File transfer: The amount of bandwidth that is used when a visitor accesses Web pages and downloads files contained on a Web site. Hosting providers place a limit on the amount of file transfer on a Web site every month and charge additional fees when file transfer exceeds the hosting plan's monthly allotment. A Web site owner who expects a large number of visitors each month should purchase a hosting package that provides a generous bandwidth allotment to avoid overage charges.

Financial management software: Applications that allow a user to collect and synthesize data from personal checking, savings, investment, and business accounts and analyze the data to make sure that personal and business finances are sound. Some financial management software programs also allow users to manage business functions such as invoicing, payroll, taxes, and customer and vendor tracking.

Hard drive: Hardware in a personal computer or server where data is stored, such as word-processor documents, media files, software files, and browser cookies. The capacity of a hard drive is expressed in gigabytes (GB). The higher the capacity of a hard drive, the more data can be stored on it. A large-capacity hard drive is essential for computers that will store large numbers of image or media files.

Hardware: Physical parts of a computer that provide various functions to make the computer operate correctly. Examples of hardware include hard drives, memory cards, processors, video cards, sound cards, CD and DVD drives, and motherboards.

High-speed Internet access: Internet access that is transmitted over a cable line or via satellite. High-speed Internet access is much quicker than dial-up — sometimes up to 50 times faster. However, high-speed Internet access subscriptions are more expensive than dial-up subscriptions and may not be available in rural or low-population areas.

Hyper Text Markup Language (HTML): A coding language used to create Web pages. HTML uses tags to tell Web browsers how to display Web site content. Popular Web site creation software automatically creates HTML as users build Web pages via a What You See Is What You Get (WYSIWYG) interface and allows users to alter the HTML code to fine-tune Web site elements.

Inbound link: A link that directs an Internet user to a Web site from a separate Web site. Inbound links are used by search engines as a factor to determine where a Web page ranks in search listings, compared to all other Web sites containing the same keywords used by a search engine user.

Internet Service Provider (ISP): A company that provides Internet service for individual or business users. ISPs often offer dial-up and high-speed Internet connection packages, based on an individual user's preferences and budget. When a user connects to the Internet, the ISP logs a series of numbers, called an IP address, which helps trace illegal or unethical activity to a particular computer.

JPEG or JPG files: An image file type that is compatible with most Internet browsers. Only static images are compatible with the JPEG format — animated images should be saved as GIF files or multimedia file types such as Flash or AVI.

Keystoning: A type of image distortion that results when a digital camera is not directly in line with the subject of the photograph, particularly when the subject is a two-dimensional object, such as a fine art painting. Keystoning makes the subject look as if one side is larger than the other or as if the top is larger or smaller than the bottom. Images that depict keystoned subjects appear unprofessional and can hinder sales.

Keyword: A word or phrase that a Web site owner believes search engine users will use when conducting a search query. When a search engine user types in a search query, the search engine finds all Web sites containing the keywords and lists them for the user. Web site owners load their site content with keywords to try to gain higher prominence in the listings returned to the user.

Keyword density: The percentage of words in a section of Web site text that is composed of keywords. Keyword density is one of the factors a search engine uses to decide where a Web page ranks in relation to all other Web sites that contain the same keywords. Most Internet marketers believe the optimal keyword density for a Web page is between 1 and 4 percent, and many marketers design Web content with a keyword density of at least 2 percent.

Link: A section of text in a Web page that is coded to direct a visitor to another page on the same Web site or a page on a different Web site, when a visitor clicks on the text. Links are coded in HTML in the format <a href="http.www.sitename.com">Click Here</a>.

Memory card: A hardware component of a personal computer that allows the computer to process software applications, operating system processes, and other common computer functions. The power of a memory card is expressed as megabytes or gigabytes of RAM — the greater the RAM, the quicker a computer can process tasks and the greater the number of tasks the computer can handle at once.

Merchant account: A special bank account used to process credit card transactions on your Web site. Merchant account providers charge setup and monthly maintenance fees for credit card acceptance and authorization services and also charge a percentage of each transaction that is processed through the merchant account.

Meta tag: A short block of text used to describe the contents of a Web page to a search engine spider. An Internet marketer may write meta tags that are composed entirely of keywords in an effort to boost a page's search engine ranking for specific keywords.

MP3: An audio file type that is commonly used to upload music and other audio to the Internet and transfer it among users. MP3 files can also easily be downloaded to iPods and other portable media devices, making them ideal for creating portable music libraries. Musicians often place MP3 files on Web sites and allow visitors to download these files for a fee.

Opt-in: A Web site visitor's acknowledgement that he or she has voluntarily subscribed to an e-mail marketing list by giving the Web site owner his or her contact information. Opt-in is also used to refer to double opt-in, a process by which a subscriber clicks a link in an e-mail to verify that he or she wishes to be included in the Web site owner's e-mail marketing list.

Outbound link: A link that directs a Web site visitor to a different Web site. Outbound links may be used to provide information to a visitor that is not available on the Web site containing the link. Internet marketers may also place outbound links to affiliate sites as a means to gain revenue.

Page title: A short block of text used to describe a Web page. In Internet Explorer browsers, the text appears in the blue bar at the top of the page. Internet marketers load page titles with keywords in an effort to boost a Web page's ranking in search engine listings for specific keywords.

PayPal: A Web site that allows online businesspeople to accept payments without a subscription to a merchant account. PayPal deducts a percentage of each payment made via its Web site and deposits the remainder into an account that sellers can withdraw from. Withdrawals from PayPal accounts can be made directly to personal or business checking accounts or via checks mailed to the sellers.

Processor: Computer hardware that is the gateway for all a computer's functions. Processors with higher power ratings assist a computer with handling tasks more quickly and processing more tasks at once.

Random Access Memory (RAM): Memory on a personal computer that is used to handle software and operating system processes. RAM is expressed in megabytes or gigabytes — the greater the amount of RAM, the more smoothly a computer can execute multiple processes.

Search directory: A compilation of Web page listings divided into multiple categories to facilitate ease of use. Web sites submitted to a search directory are reviewed and categorized by human editors rather than search engine spiders. As a result, search directory users may find more relevant results in directory listings than in search engine listings.

Search engine: A Web site that allows users to enter keywords to find sites with content relevant to their search. Search engines use programs called spiders to read, evaluate, and index Web pages for inclusion into the search engine's database.

Search engine optimization (SEO): A process of refining content on a Web page, blog, or article to include keywords in the optimal density and placement for high rankings in search engines. SEO also uses link building in an effort to improve rankings for a particular Web page or Web site.

Site map: A Web page or document that contains a complete listing of all the domain's Web site pages and subpages. Site maps can be useful for visitors who are unfamiliar with navigating a complex Web site. Site maps also help Web site owners ensure all pages on a Web site are being reviewed and indexed by search engine spiders.

Social marketing: A marketing strategy that uses social networking Web sites, such as MySpace, De.licio.us, Digg, and Facebook to promote products and services. The content placed on these sites is primarily informational and may contain links to the owner's Web site or other promotional content elsewhere on the Internet.

Software: Programs that are designed to allow a computer to perform certain functions. Examples of software include games, Web site creation tools, finance applications, and word-processing programs.

Sound card: Computer hardware that allows audio files to be played on a computer's built-in or external speakers. Higher-quality sound cards reproduce audio that is closer to true stereo sound than stock sound cards included with commonly available computer system packages. A high-quality sound card is essential for musicians who sell their songs or compilations via the Internet.

Spam: An unsolicited e-mail message sent by a person

or business to gain sales, transmit viruses, or carry out other questionable activity. Transmission of spam violates United States federal law, and prolific use of spam can result in fines and imprisonment of the sender.

Spider: A software application used by search engines to review and index Web pages for inclusion in its search engine listings. Spiders can read Web page text and links but cannot read images. Search engine spiders regularly scour the Internet for new content; however, a Web site owner can submit his site to search engines to have his or her site reviewed and indexed by search engine spiders more quickly.

Terms of Use: The rules decided on by the owner or administrator of a Web site or discussion board regarding how users may and may not add information to the site or use the information contained within the site. Users who violate the terms of use may have their content removed from the site and may be banned from the site for intentional or repeated violations.

Traffic: The number of visitors that access a Web page during a specified period. The higher the traffic received by a Web page, the more popular it is and the more useful it is for generating sales and e-mail marketing subscriptions.

Universal Resource Locator (URL): A designated name that allows Web browsers to find a specific Web page via the Internet. Each page of a Web site is assigned a specific URL that cannot be used by any other Web page, whether part of the same Web site or a different Web site.

Video card: Computer hardware that allows images on a computer or on the Internet to be displayed on the computer's monitor. High-quality video cards produce higher resolution, greater image clarity, and smoother animation than stock video cards included with commonly available computer system packages. A high-quality video card is essential for graphic artists and other visual artists who sell their creative works on the Internet.

Web host: A provider that allows a Web site owner to store Web site files on its server and allows users to access those files from that server. Web hosts may also offer a number of other services to assist Web site owners in publishing a fully functional Web site, such as CGI bins, Web site templates, or site creation software.

Web page: A part of a Web site that has a specific URL that is unique to that page. Web pages may be used to separate Web site content that is used for different purposes, such as art

gallery pages, contact pages, and FAQ pages.

Web site: A dedicated collection of pages on the Internet that are connected to each other and are used to promote a business, make products and services available to Internet users, or provide information about a particular topic or interest. Individual pages that comprise a Web site are assigned specific URLs that uniquely identify the pages and allow users to find the pages via an Internet browser, search engine, or search directory.

Web site creation software: A software application that allows a user to design and create his or her own Web site without the assistance of a professional Web designer or programmer. Some Web site creation software packages, such as those commonly offered by Web site hosting providers, offer templates a Web site owner can customize to create his or her Web site. Other Web site creation software uses a WYSIWYG interface that allows users to drag and drop elements to provide a greater level of customization. Software that uses a WYSIWYG interface also often provides access to a Web site's HTML code, so users can fine-tune the design and content of their Web pages.

interface to ease the creation of Web pages without knowledge of HTML or other Web site coding languages. Through a WYSIWYG interface, users can drag and drop elements such as text, graphics, and video into a Web page markup, and the software will automatically generate the HTML code necessary to display the Web page on an Internet browser.

Wi-Fi: Wireless Internet access, which is accessed by a wireless card included with many laptop computers. Wi-Fi may be accessed from a signal provided by a wireless router connected to a desktop computer or from a satellite transmission hosted by a large ISP. Many restaurants and coffee shops in the United States now offer free Wi-Fi access to patrons as a means of attracting and retaining customers.

What You See Is What You Get (WYSIWYG): Popular Web site creation software titles offer users a WYSIWIG

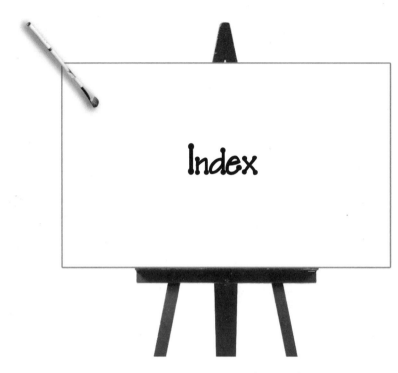

Index